ALL ABOUT...

..Aliens

**FOR ALIEN ENTHUSIASTS AND SCEPTICS ALIKE, THIS BOOK
TAKES A KEEN LOOK AT THE TOPIC OF EXTRA TERRESTRIALS**

CH LEE

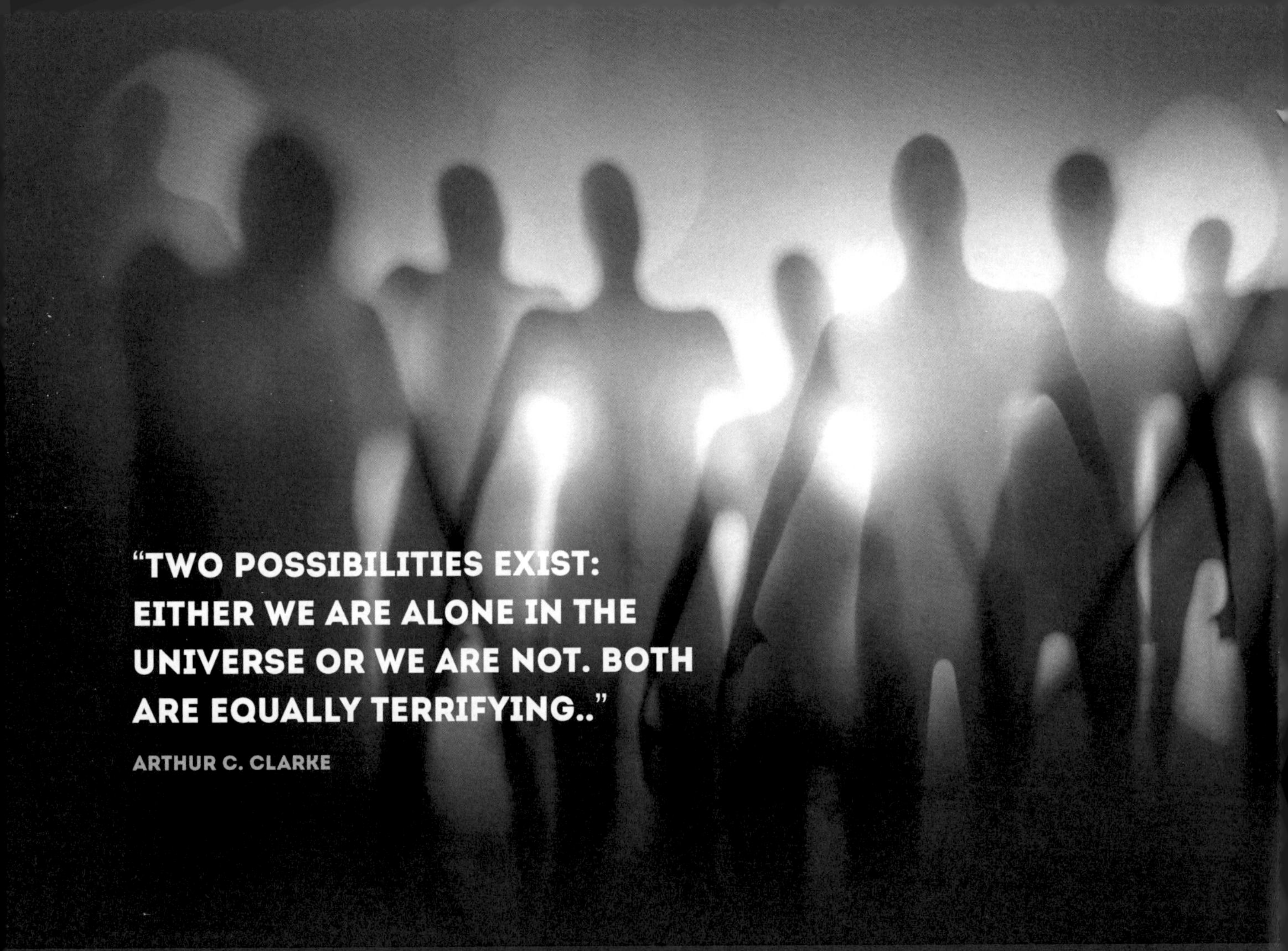

"TWO POSSIBILITIES EXIST:
EITHER WE ARE ALONE IN THE
UNIVERSE OR WE ARE NOT. BOTH
ARE EQUALLY TERRIFYING.."

ARTHUR C. CLARKE

ALL ABOUT...

..Aliens

FOR ALIEN ENTHUSIASTS AND SCEPTICS ALIKE, THIS BOOK TAKES A KEEN LOOK AT THE TOPIC OF EXTRA TERRESTRIALS

CH LEE

"THE UNIVERSE IS A PRETTY BIG PLACE. IF IT'S JUST US, SEEMS LIKE AN AWFUL WASTE OF SPACE."

CARL SAGAN

CONTENTS

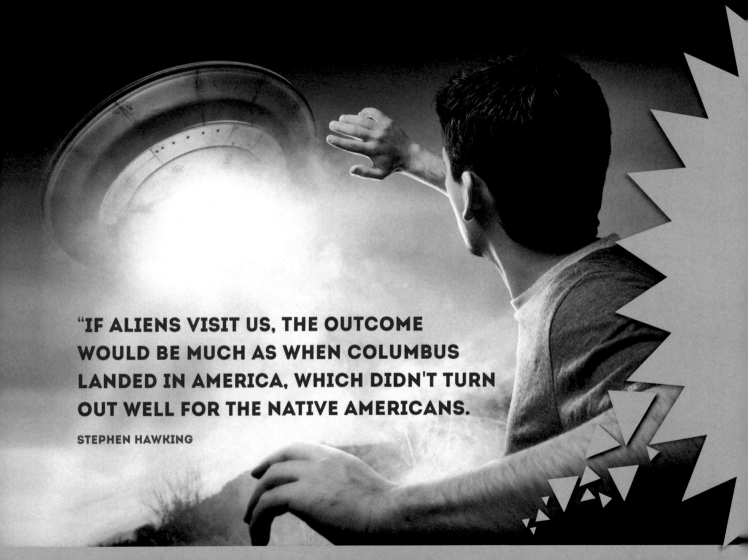

"IF ALIENS VISIT US, THE OUTCOME WOULD BE MUCH AS WHEN COLUMBUS LANDED IN AMERICA, WHICH DIDN'T TURN OUT WELL FOR THE NATIVE AMERICANS.

STEPHEN HAWKING

INTRODUCTION

Interest in the possibility that we share the universe with other intelligent beings has reached fever pitch with the discovery in the last few years that the universe is positively stuffed with planets, some of which are sure to be very similar to Earth. What is the truth about the creatures which must surely lurk Out There? Are they likely to resemble the green-skinned monsters of science fiction, or perhaps take some unexpected, unrecognisable form? Or could they be rather like us? And what about the sixty-four thousand dollar question - could we visit them? Or at least communicate with them?

So far no one knows the answers to any of these questions for sure, and perhaps we never will - until we either get that call from the stars we have been waiting for, or find a way to travel across the unspeakably vast interstellar gulf.

However, while we're waiting we can make some pretty good guesses. We are the generation which began the exploration of space, sending our probes across the solar system and in a couple of cases, out beyond it. We are the first generation in humankind's millions of years of history to know that the surface of Mars looks like a pinky-brown builder's yard, that the Jovian moon Europa has a vast and turbulent hidden ocean, and most recently that the universe has planets by the quintillion.

These are exciting times to be around. There can only be more surprises in the future. This book will point the way towards where they may come from.

1

MYTHS AND MYSTERIES

'IF ONE COULD KNOW WHETHER AMONG THAT GLITTERING HOST THERE WERE HERE AND THERE OTHER SPIRIT–INHABITED GRAINS OF ROCK AND METAL'

OLAF STAPLEDON, STARMAKER (1937)

Alien life, extra-terrestrials, beings from other worlds - it is hard to think of a subject on which we have so many questions and so few answers. Are there really other intelligent life forms living out their lives somewhere in the vast void beyond our own cosy little planet? Where might we find them, and how? Have they visited us? Could we visit them – or at least communicate with them?

This book is a common-sense attempt to explain what we know, what we don't know and what we might be able to find out in answer to those questions. It has been written not by a ufologist or a committed believer in aliens, nor by a cautious scientist with a reputation to protect, but by a thinking science enthusiast who has been examining these questions for many years.

THE INVENTION OF ALIENS

The idea that Earth might not be the only place where intelligent life is found can be dated back to Copernicus, the 16th century astronomer who first announced that our planet was not at the centre of the universe. Copernicus's claim marked the beginning of a scientific revolution. As the centuries went by and telescopes and cosmological theory developed hand in hand, we humans realised not only that the Earth is an ordinary planet orbiting an ordinary star but that our star is one of billions in a galaxy which is in turn one among countless billions.

The Italian philosopher Giordano Bruno was one of those who suggested that the universe must contain other solar systems and other life-bearing planets. In 1600 Bruno was burned at the stake for this and other heresies, but he spoke for the future. By the 18th century many astronomers shared Bruno's view, among them William Herschel, the man who discovered the seventh planet, Uranus. However Herschel's claim that every astronomical body, even the sun, must harbour alien life forms did little for his reputation as a man of sober judgment.

Meanwhile literature was beginning to explore the concept of alien races on other worlds. Jonathan Swift's *Gulliver's Travels* (1726) was an early example of something very like science fiction, featuring as it did a variety of strange races of humanoids, including a master race of mathematicians living in a land floating in the heavens.

The sky according to Copernicus

statue of Giordano Bruno at the Campo de' Fiori, Rome

THE BIRTH OF SCIENCE FICTION

The concept of aliens as superior beings capable of invading Earth and subjugating the human race is a more recent development, emerging in the latter part of the 19th century. In the half-century before the outbreak of the First World War more than 60 works of fiction were published which dealt with invasions of Great Britain. The main focus was on threats from other nations, particularly Germany. One book, however, took a much more interesting idea as its theme; the idea of an invasion by creatures from another planet. This was H G Wells' *The War Of The Worlds*, published in 1898.

With *The War Of The Worlds* and his other stories, notably *The Time Machine*, *The Invisible Man* and *The First Men In The Moon*, Wells can reasonably be credited with giving birth to the modern science fiction genre. Although a handful of books dealing with alien worlds had been published before, Wells'

work was in a different class. So vividly told was his story of a Martian invasion, so detailed the description, so plausible the science, that it became an instant classic. In fact, 116 years on, it has never been out of print.

In 1938, on the eve of the Second World War, the book was given extra notoriety by a radio dramatisation on a US radio station narrated and directed by the actor Orson Welles. In a style far ahead of its time, the story was presented like a live news report, as if it was an authentic broadcast of real-life events. Thousands of listeners were terrified out of their wits, believing, understandably, that the Martians really had landed. This helped to ensure lasting fame for the book, the narrator and Mars itself.

THE 'CANALS' OF MARS

While the scientific world in general continued to remain cautious on the question of alien life, there were exceptions.

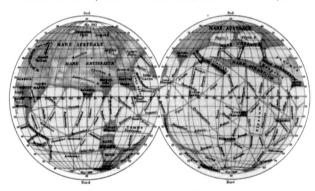

Carte d'ensemble de la planéte Mars
avec ses lignes sombres non doublées
observées pendant les six oppositions de 1877-1888
par J.V.Schiaparelli

Atlas of Mars by Giovanni Schiaparelli, made in 1888.
Note that this is a South-Up map; the South Pole is on top.

One of the most notable was the American astronomer Percival Lowell (1855-1916), who founded the Lowell Observatory in Flagstaff, Arizona. Lowell was much taken by the work of an Italian astronomer, Giovanni Schiaparelli, who claimed in the 1870s that he could see *canali* (channels) on the surface of Mars. Unfortunately *canali* was mistranslated into English as

Percival Lowell

'canals'. Lowell seems to have put two and two together and made seventeen. When he turned his new telescope on Mars in 1894, he was convinced that he could indeed see canals, and produced a series of sketches of them which have been held up to ridicule ever since. The sketches appeared to show a network of ruler-straight waterways criss-crossing the Red Planet. Surely this was evidence that Mars was peopled by intelligent beings who had created the 'canals' to irrigate their dried-up world? Lowell wrote two popular books to advance this point of view.

Unfortunately, as telescopes improved, the canals disappeared. They were exposed as a combination of optical illusion (the human eye's talent for pattern recognition, with the brain eagerly joining up dots to make non-existent straight lines)

Isaac Asimov

John Wyndham

Ray Bradbury

Arthur C Clarke

Fred Hoyle

A few of the great authors of classic science fiction

and wishful thinking. It's a pity Lowell is chiefly remembered for his imaginary canals, because in fact he was a fine astronomer, whose work eventually led to the discovery of the ninth planet, Pluto (now demoted to minor planet status).

THE SCI FI BOOM

It didn't take much for such ideas to seize the minds of the public. By the 1920s there was a thriving pulp magazine industry in the USA retailing all manner of stories about alien beings inhabiting outlandish worlds. National consciousness of the threat of invasion from aliens in the broadest sense on both sides of the Atlantic ensured that as the 20th century continued, the focus of science fiction was firmly on aliens as

evil beings of superior intelligence, usually physically repulsive.

As the century wore on and the science fiction genre became more sophisticated, great sci-fi writers like Arthur C Clarke, Ray Bradbury, Fred Hoyle, Isaac Asimov and John Wyndham painted compelling and realistic pictures of how life beyond Earth might actually work. Star Trek, for all its cheerful disregard of the laws of physics, helped to turn the tide against the idea of aliens as evil invaders by placing most of the races encountered by the crew of the Starship *Enterprise* on the moral high ground.

THE PSEUDOSCIENCE GRAVY TRAIN

Science fiction, whether fanciful or realistic, is all good clean fun, but a number of authors have made a killing from writing

Pyramids at Giza

Nazca lines in Peru

Zark's Factoid

Although Fred Hoyle wrote some of the most compelling sci-fi novels in the literature, he did not even mention them in his autobiography - he preferred to be remembered for his considerable scientific achievements.

supposedly factual books about aliens, particularly ancient ones. Perhaps the doyen of these is the Swiss author Erich von Däniken, who in the 1960s and 70s wrote a series of best-selling books claiming that Earth has been visited in the past by aliens who, among other achievements, laid out the famous Nazca lines in Peru and helped to build the Pyramids. The income from the books made von Däniken a lot of money, which at least enabled him to repay his debts following a series of convictions for fraud. Even von Däniken himself has admitted that much of what he wrote was wrong or fabricated.

CROP CIRCLES

Von Däniken's claims were followed by the famous crop circle sightings from the 1970s on, when complex geometric shapes started appearing overnight in fields of standing crops in southern England. For years the world speculated about their origins, until in 1991 two men, Doug Bower and Dave Chorley, revealed that they had been

responsible and demonstrated how they had done it. After this a veritable crop circle industry grew up across the Western World, as others realised that anyone could make their own crop circles, and some profited from the attention. Yet even today, many are reluctant to let go of their belief that aliens have been responsible for at least some of the designs; a quick trawl of the internet will reveal countless organisations which are determined to link crop circles to alien beings, even though the techniques behind them have been fully explained, and it does not seem to have occurred to the aliens to start making crop circles until they saw the work of Bower and Chorley.

'Oi Zark! Why didn't we think of this before? Doug and Dave are legends'

VISITORS FROM SPACE?

By the time space travel became a reality in the 1960s, many ordinary people took it for granted that there were aliens out there and that they had in all probability already popped in, many times, to see us on Earth.

This belief reached its peak following the notorious Roswell incident. In 1947, an airborne object of some kind crashed on a ranch near Roswell, New Mexico. Little was made of the incident at the time and it was forgotten about until 1978, when Major Jesse Marcel, who had been involved in recovering the debris, told a 'ufologist', Stanton T Friedman, that he believed that the military had in fact found and recovered the wreckage of an alien spacecraft. This was too good a story for the popular press to ignore, particularly when in 1989 a former mortician called Glenn Dennis claimed alien autopsies had

been carried out at the Roswell base. Dennis' accounts have been accused of inconsistency. In 1991 he co-founded a successful museum dedicated to the UFO claims.

The United States Armed Forces maintain that all they recovered near Roswell was debris from the crash of an experimental high-altitude surveillance balloon belonging to what was then a classified program named Mogul. In contrast, the UFO devotees have chosen to believe Jesse Marcel and Glenn Dennis, maintaining that an alien craft really was found and its occupants captured. The military, say the UFO disciples, covered it all up. Well they would, wouldn't they? A story like Roswell is too good to be discredited, or allowed to die.

As the author can attest from having worked in the newspaper industry, popular newspapers are adept at turning hearsay and hypothesis into light-hearted 'news'. You don't have to produce a shred of evidence that a flying saucer landed in Kensington Gardens on Sunday afternoon to run a story about it; you simply have to find someone who is willing to say they saw it (even if everybody else says they didn't and the experts say they couldn't have). Many people seem to be willing to embroider and fabricate for fifteen minutes of fame – or perhaps they just tell reporters what they want to hear. The two little words no reporter ever wants to tell his editor are 'no story'.

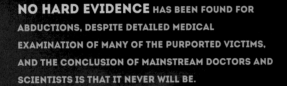

NO HARD EVIDENCE HAS BEEN FOUND FOR
ABDUCTIONS, DESPITE DETAILED MEDICAL
EXAMINATION OF MANY OF THE PURPORTED VICTIMS,
AND THE CONCLUSION OF MAINSTREAM DOCTORS AND
SCIENTISTS IS THAT IT NEVER WILL BE.

ALIEN ABDUCTIONS

Late on the evening of September 19 1961, a New Hampshire couple, Betty and Barney Hill, were driving back from holiday along a lonely mountain road when Betty spotted a bright point of light which appeared to be moving upwards from the horizon. Barney stopped the car and they took a closer look. Through binoculars, Barney saw an object which at first appeared to be a plane, but which then changed shape and descended. They

Betty and Barney Hill

stopped the car in the highway, with the strange craft, which appeared flat and circular, hovering just above the car.

Barney got out of the car and saw a group of figures in glossy black outfits looking out of the windows of the craft. One of them telepathically sent him an instruction to stay where he was, and a structure was lowered from the base of the craft. Barney ran back to the car in a panic and the pair drove off at speed, the car being

BETTY AND BARNEY HILL INCIDENT

On the night of September 19-20, 1961, Portsmouth, NH couple Betty and Barney Hill experienced a close encounter with an unidentified flying object and two hours of "lost" time while driving south on Rte 3 near Lincoln. They filed an official Air Force Project Blue Book report of a brightly-lit cigar-shaped craft the next day, but were not public with their story until it was leaked in the Boston Traveler in 1965. This was the first widely-reported UFO abduction report in the United States.

assaulted by strange vibrations and buzzing sounds which seemed to interfere with their memories over the next few hours.

The next morning the Hills, still confused by their experience, found that their watches had stopped working and their clothes and shoes had been damaged. Night after night they began to experience peculiar dreams.

The couple reported their experiences to the local US air force base, and the real fun began. Over the years investigations have been conducted, books have been written and TV documentaries made to try to establish what really happened to the Hills, without a satisfactory conclusion. Dr Benjamin Simon, who hypnotised the couple in an attempt to get to the bottom of it, concluded that Barney's story was a fantasy inspired by Betty's reports of her dreams in the period after the incident.

The Hill case sparked off a wave of reports of alien abductions or abduction attempts over the following decades, now running into thousands. A 1992 poll showed that no fewer than four million Americans believed they had been abducted by aliens, many of them claiming to have been intimately examined, usually sexually, before being returned to safety, usually dazed and traumatised but without a mark on them. One wonders what the aliens would do with all those people, and why they were all returned to Earth with intact memories but with no tangible traces of their ordeal.

Who we abducting tonight Zark?

Can't we just get a Curry and a DVD this evening?

9

No hard evidence has been found for abductions, despite detailed medical examination of many of the purported victims, and the conclusion of mainstream doctors and scientists is that it never will be; these experiences are thought to be the product of false memory syndrome, sleep paralysis, psychopathology and/or some form of post-traumatic stress disorder. A notable factor is the resemblance of the abductors and their craft to aliens recently portrayed on television (the aliens described by Barney Hill closely resembled those shown in an episode of *The Outer Limits* only twelve days before the incident). It can be no coincidence that there were virtually no reports of alien encounters before the TV age. Odd that ET should have decided to start visiting us just after television was invented and that he should nearly always target the USA, the cradle of TV sci-fi.

The late physicist Carl Sagan has this to say about alien abductions and experimentation in his enlightening book *The Demon-Haunted World*: "Why should beings so advanced in physics and engineering, crossing vast interstellar distances, be so backward when it comes to biology? Why are the examining instruments so reminiscent of what can be found at the neighbourhood clinic? Why go to all the trouble of repeated sexual encounters... why not steal a few egg and sperm cells, read the genetic code, and then manufacture as many copies as you like?"

Carl Sagan

THE NEED TO BELIEVE

Star Trek must be one of the least realistic of sci-fi productions of modern times, treated with amused indulgence by those outside its fan base. Yet it had, and has, an adoring following numbering many millions of devoted 'Trekkies' around the world. In March 1997 a more sinister side to fandom revealed itself when all 39 members of a cult called Heaven's Gate poisoned themselves, believing the Earth was about to be 'recycled' and that through suicide they would be rescued by an alien spacecraft. They were obsessive Trekkies.

It seems we all want to believe in aliens, and that while for most people speculating about possible contact with them is merely an interesting topic of dinner-table conversation, for others it is a life-and-death matter.

THE TROUBLE WITH SPACE TOURISM

If the ET enthusiasts are right, Earth is regularly visited by voyagers from the stars. Yet, as we'll hear in more detail in a later chapter, there are some very serious practical objections to this idea.

Space is ridiculously big. Our nearest planet, Venus, is (at its closest) one million times further away from Earth than Guildford is from London. Our nearest star, Proxima Centauri, is a million times further away than Venus. Our nearest major galaxy, Andromeda, is half a million times further away than Proxima Centauri. These distances are literally unimaginable.

Are we there yet?

EARTH 1,000,000,000,000, 000,000,000,000,000, 000,000,000 Miles

Zark's Factoid...
The Andromeda Galaxy is approaching the Milky Way at approximately 100 to 140 kilometres per second. It is the most distant object in the sky that you can see with your unaided eye

the Andromeda Galaxy

For reasons we'll be looking at later, it is extremely unlikely that intelligent beings inhabit any other body in our own solar system. The nearest place our alien visitors could be coming from would be the nearest star which might just harbour a life-supporting planet. To find that, you will have to travel well beyond Proxima Centauri, perhaps to somewhere like the red dwarf star Gliese 581, now known to have several broadly Earth-like planets in orbit around it.

Gliese 581 is 20 light years from Earth, or nearly five times the distance of Proxima Centauri. It would take a spacecraft of the kind used in the current programme of solar system exploration around 300,000 years to get there. And in galactic terms that's just popping next door – crossing the galaxy would take the best part of a billion years.

Obviously our aliens are not going to be dropping in every week if journeys like that are involved – unless they have found a method of transport which is millions of times faster than anything we know about. The reasons why this is very unlikely will be discussed later.

2 MESSAGES FROM OTHER WORLDS

'FOR ALL THE NIGHT, I HEARD THE THIN GNAT-VOICES CRY, STAR TO FAINT STAR, ACROSS THE SKY'

RUPERT BROOKE, THE JOLLY COMPANY

The search for life on other worlds began in earnest one day in April 1960, when a young astronomer called Frank Drake pointed a giant radio telescope at the star Tau Ceti, 11 light years from Earth and therefore one of our nearest neighbours. This was the start of Project Ozma, the first chapter in SETI – the Search for Extra-Terrestrial Intelligence.

Frank Drake

The idea of SETI was, and is, to examine likely nearby star systems for any sign of radio transmissions, deliberate or incidental. Drake reasoned that if there were other civilisations around in our neck of the Galaxy, they might be sending out radio signals which we Earthlings could listen to, as radio penetrates our atmosphere (and presumably those of other worlds) with little attenuation. He knew it was a long shot, but success would have been world changing.

As early as 1896, the electrical engineering pioneer Nikola Tesla had suggested that radio could be used to make contact with other worlds. In 1899, while investigating atmospheric electricity, Tesla observed a series of repetitive signals which he interpreted as being of extraterrestrial origin; he suggested that they were coming from Mars. No one still imagines he was right about that, but it started the ball rolling.

In the early 1900s, Guglielmo Marconi and Lord Kelvin suggested that radio could be used to contact Martians, and Marconi even claimed that his stations had picked up signals from the Red Planet.

In 1924, when Mars was in a particularly favourable opposition (opposite the sun in the sky, as seen from Earth, and at its closest to us), an attempt was made in the USA to listen in to any radio signals the hypothetical Martians might be broadcasting. A radio receiver was hung to an airship and lifted 10,000 feet above the ground. The chief cryptographer of the US Army was even assigned to translate any Martian messages. A day of radio silence was ordained. Nothing was heard.

The SETI researchers decided to 'listen' on the 21cm wavelength (also known as the 1420 MHz frequency) emitted by the clouds of

Cover of sheet music for 'A Signal from Mars' inspired by the interception of radio signals believed to have come from Mars.

hydrogen which are found across the universe. They hypothesised that this wavelength was significant because it would be recognised by intelligent beings everywhere in the universe for its association with hydrogen, and it made sense, if you wanted to communicate with another civilisation, to attract their attention by using a number with universal significance – just as using the number 3.142 would tell any race which had discovered geometry that you knew about pi (π), the ratio of the circumference of a circle to its diameter.

So how do we know that there is anyone out there sending radio messages in the first place? What happens if we are all alone in the galaxy?

THE DRAKE EQUATION

Frank Drake has given his name to one of the most famous ideas in cosmology – the Drake Equation, a formula for estimating the number of worlds within our galaxy with which radio communication might be possible.

$$N = N^* \, fs \, fp \, ne \, fi \, fc \, fL$$

The factors in the equation are, in order:

N = the number of civilisations sending out radio signals now

N^* = number of stars in the Milky Way galaxy

fs = fraction of the above which are sun-like

fp = the fraction of stars with planets

ne = planets in a star's habitable zone

fi = the fraction of potentially life-bearing planets which produce life

fc = the fraction of civilisations ever inhabited by intelligent beings

fl = percentage of a planetary lifetime during which a communicating civilisation exists.

Drake was not making any particular claims about the value of N. He just thought it would be a useful starting point for a debate, and he was right about that. His equation, and variations of it, are still being discussed.

The Drake equation will never be able to tell us with any accuracy how many civilisations are 'out there', because we can barely guess at the values for the last few factors.

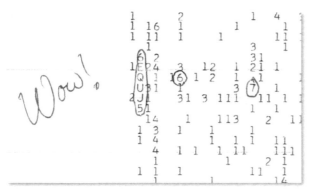

A scan of a color copy of the original computer printout, taken several years after the 1977 arrival of the **Wow!** signal.

THE 'WOW' SIGNAL

The SETI researchers trawled the skies without success for more than 17 years, until one day a signal came through that stopped the investigators in their tracks. The instrument in use was the Big Ear radio telescope of Ohio State University, which was fixed, so it swept the sky in time with the Earth's rotation. The signal reached a peak intensity 30 times stronger than the background noise of deep space, and corresponded almost exactly to the 21cm wavelength. The signal has become known as the 'Wow!' signal because its discoverer, Jerry Ehman, wrote 'Wow!' on the printout. It behaved as you would expect a strong, continuous static transmission source to behave, lasting throughout the 72 seconds it took for the telescope to pass the source. The point of origin was calculated to be a point in the constellation Sagittarius, not associated with any obvious star.

The researchers waited, hearts in mouths, for the next sweep of the telescope, but this time they saw nothing out of the ordinary. Other investigators turned their instruments on the co-ordinates and also drew a blank. Despite careful searching, the Wow! signal has never been seen again. No one has managed to come up with a convincing theory for its origin.

SETI has now been operating across various countries, using a widening range of techniques, almost continuously since 1960. In 1993 the US Congress pulled the plug on funding, but the baton was taken up by the SETI League and the SETI Institute, aided by grants and donations and urged on by a growing number of amateur enthusiasts. By the time it had been running for 50 years several thousand stars within around 100 light years of Earth had been studied, and its scope is widening by the week.

Zark's Factoid...

Jodie Foster, who played fictional SETI scientist Ellie Arroway in the 1997 movie 'Contact', helped raise (along with other supporters), funds to operate the Allen Telescope Array for another year which is used by SETI.

However nothing else as striking as the Wow! signal has yet been found, and certainly no evidence of other civilisations.

Hope has by no means been abandoned. The project has become increasingly complex and sophisticated, covering more and more wavebands and reaching out further into the galaxy. While the scientific community in general has remained sceptical, public interest has been such that SETI is now able to operate on many fronts. Project Argus co-ordinates around 140 home dishes of 3-5m diameter, each of which, thanks to improvements in technology, is as sensitive as the original Big Ear dish which detected the Wow! signal. For the enthusiast who doesn't happen to have a fifteen-foot radio dish at his or her disposal, SETI@home enables anyone with a computer to take part by running a programme on their desktop PC to analyse a small chunk of the vast quantities of data gathered by the professionals' radio telescopes.

Jodrell Bank - The University of Manchester UK

The sensitivity of our radio telescopes is now such that we could pick up faint signals from a very long way away. The traditional single steerable dish telescope, such as that exemplified for many years by the 250-foot Lovell telescope at Jodrell Bank in Cheshire, is giving way to much larger structures which are made up of a number of separate telescopes working together. The Square Kilometre Array (SKA), now under construction by an international venture, will take this to a dramatically new level. It will consist of 3000 interconnected dishes with a total area of a square kilometre, all perfectly synchronised. The dishes are being sited in desert areas of Australia and South Africa, where the skies are clear and terrestrial radio interference is minimal. Though the SKA's main purpose is radio astronomy rather than the detection of alien transmissions, it will be listening out for them – and it will be able to pick up the equivalent of a mobile phone call 50 light years away.

The SKA-MID will comprise of both tile based aperture array telescopes, which will be able to electronically point at multiple regions of the sky at the same time, and 15m wide dish telescopes
(SKA Organisation)

BROADCASTING TO THE STARS

What about the other way round – the possibility of aliens listening to us? It is now almost a century since regular radio broadcasts began on Earth, so there is an expanding sphere of radio and television transmission centred on the solar system, currently with a radius approaching 100 light years (a phenomenon beautifully portrayed by the prologue to the sci-fi film Contact, based on the book by the late Carl Sagan, charismatic planetary physicist and SETI champion). Already several hundred stars are being gently washed by the waves of our electronic chatter. Are there planets around those stars? We now know that there are, probably thousands of them. Does anyone live there and have the capability of listening? Possibly – though probably not, for reasons which we will discuss.

Under a programme called 'Active SETI' there have been attempts to send deliberate messages to the stars. The Pioneer 10 and 11 spacecraft and Voyager 1 and 2 are all now heading out of the solar system armed with plaques bearing engraved information about their home planet. In 1974 the Arecibo radio telescope broadcast a pictorial message directed at Messier 13, a globular cluster on the outskirts

Illustration of Voyager 1
(Courtesy of NASA/JPL)

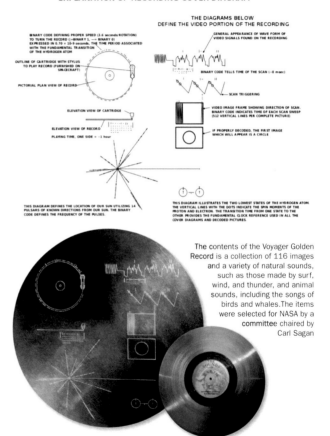

The contents of the Voyager Golden Record is a collection of 116 images and a variety of natural sounds, such as those made by surf, wind, and thunder, and animal sounds, including the songs of birds and whales.The items were selected for NASA by a committee chaired by Carl Sagan

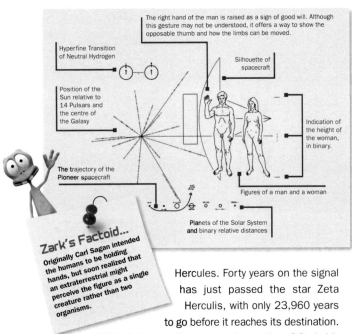

The right hand of the man is raised as a sign of good will. Although this gesture may not be understood, it offers a way to show the opposable thumb and how the limbs can be moved.

Hyperfine Transition of Neutral Hydrogen

Silhouette of spacecraft

Position of the Sun relative to 14 Pulsars and the centre of the Galaxy

Indication of the height of the woman, in binary.

The trajectory of the Pioneer spacecraft

Figures of a man and a woman

Planets of the Solar System and binary relative distances

Hercules. Forty years on the signal has just passed the star Zeta Herculis, with only 23,960 years to go before it reaches its destination. Will it find an audience when it gets there? Probably not – globular clusters are built of old stars which were made before most of the heavy elements in the universe had been created by supernovae, and without heavy elements there is unlikely to be life.

Many still argue that SETI is a waste of time and money, either because the world has better things to do with its resources or because, as many scientists believe, it is doomed to failure. Are they right? What are the problems with SETI?

EXPLAINING THE EERIE SILENCE

First of all, most SETI work is still very limited in range. In the context of the Milky Way, a hundred light years is an absurdly small distance. The SETI project for most of its history has been the equivalent of searching for a lost contact lens on a football pitch by examining only the area covered by your boot. Far fewer than one millionth of all the stars in the Galaxy, which is roughly 100,000 light years in diameter and contains at least 200 billion stars, lie within a hundred light years.

Secondly, the radio age is probably only a passing flicker on cosmic timescales. We invented radio transmission barely a century ago, and there is no reason to think we will go on using it indefinitely – and even if we do, how long will our civilisation last? Even in the extraordinary eventuality that we manage to keep ourselves functioning and broadcasting for another million years, that would be only about one ten-thousandth of the age of the Milky Way. If other civilisations do arise over the multibillion-year history of our galaxy, the chances of them broadcasting just when we happen to be listening out for them must be exceedingly small. The SETI radio telescopes can only detect that infinitesimal proportion of intelligent races which happen to be on air while we are tuned in.

Thirdly, SETI relies on the hope that other civilisations will want to advertise their presence. The human urge to communicate with the unknown may not be shared by other beings, and more advanced civilisations than ours may have decided it is more prudent to observe radio silence. Perhaps they have developed more subtle methods of communication which cannot be picked up by eavesdroppers.

Looking on the bright side, SETI is becoming vastly more powerful and listening in to thousands more worlds with every passing year, so the odds are falling. The days have gone when SETI was confined to a few radio frequencies. We now have computer technology which enables us to search thousands of wavebands automatically, and the sensitivity of our instruments, even before the Square Kilometre Array is ready, could pick up signals from much further away. Since the development of the laser we have also started to search for high-intensity light pulses, which might be the preferred method of communication for post-radio civilisations.

THE DANGERS OF MAKING CONTACT

Thrilling as the thought of contacting other civilisations is, the dangers of success cannot be overlooked. The early portrayal of aliens as loathsome predators and invaders gave way in the 1960s and 70s to the idea that extraterrestrials would prove wise and benign beings whose intervention in our affairs was designed to save us from

our profligacy and warmongering and set us on the path of righteousness. This theme has been explored in countless sci-fi **books** and films. Yet the nature of life itself **should** remind us that alien beings may **not** be like that at all. All the creatures we see about us on our planet are utterly, mindlessly selfish, dedicated only to the survival of their own species – that's how life works, through blind evolution driven by competition. Birds eat spiders, spiders **eat** flies and fly larvae eat caterpillars **from the** inside. Poachers kill elephants for their tusks and elephants graze jungles to destruction. Big fish eat small fish and small fish eat smaller fish. Why should our hypothetical aliens be any different? They too must have evolved through ruthless competition.

And yet it seems unlikely that creatures with the capacity to travel or communicate between the stars would be slavering monsters whose only interest is killing. Homo sapiens is the first terrestrial species to have tackled space flight, and the first with the intelligence and self-awareness to start thinking beyond its own day-to-day needs and consider the good of the world it lives in. Greed may rule, but at least, now that our activities are beginning to threaten the very planet we live on, some of us are thinking about our responsibility to it. Perhaps a more advanced race would have taken this further, and be thinking about the good of the galaxy, of the universe. Perhaps when ET comes knocking he really will be hoping to save us, not eat us and steal our planet.

So why hasn't he come knocking already?

THE FERMI PARADOX

In 1950 the great physicist Enrico Fermi posed a very interesting question about the possibility of alien life: **'Where is everybody?'** It had occurred to him that if other civilisations arose with reasonable frequency within our galaxy, the earlier ones should have had plenty of time to get to us by now – after all, the galaxy has been around for something like ten billion years and star systems containing the heavy elements necessary for life have been available for most of that time. An intelligent race which developed, say, a billion years ago should have long since achieved extraordinary technological

Enrico Fermi

feats, including, one would imagine, both space travel and the detection of other inhabited worlds – worlds like ours.

Perhaps advanced life really is extremely rare. Perhaps it is the usual fate of species which get too clever and powerful to drive themselves to extinction within a few thousand years. Or perhaps interstellar travel, for a living organism, is truly as hopelessly difficult as it seems from our perspective on 21st century Earth; perhaps it is beyond anything a carbon-based life form can hope for.

For many decades, the conventional position on extraterrestrial life has been that the sun is just an ordinary star in an ordinary part of an ordinary galaxy, and that there is nothing special about the earth except that it is about the right distance from its parent star and about the right size to support life. We humans are nothing special, is the claim, and there are probably millions of races across the universe which are at least as advanced as we are.

That picture is changing. As we begin to understand more about the earth, we are beginning to realise that in fact it is a remarkable place, and that while superficially earth-like planets may be common, those with the particular properties that allow advanced life to develop are probably very rare indeed.

Zark's Factoid...

Voyager 1 has been travelling through space at 38,000 miles per hour, and after 37 years of travel it has only just left the outermost reaches of our Solar System. Going at that speed, it wouldn't reach another star for 100,000 years!

Anybody there?... hello!...cooey... Anybody?

NASA, ESA, and the Hubble Heritage (STScI/AURA)-ESA/Hubble Collaboration

3 SEARCHING FOR LIFE IN THE SOLAR SYSTEM

"ALL THESE WORLDS ARE YOURS. EXCEPT EUROPA. ATTEMPT NO LANDING THERE." SO WARNED THE PROTECTORS OF LIFE ON JUPITER'S ICY MOON IN 2010

2061: ODYSSEY THREE, BY ARTHUR C. CLARKE (1987)

Until the 1960s, we knew the other planets and their moons only from faint, blurred images in telescopes and on photographic plates. It was clear that the giant outer planets, Jupiter, Saturn, Uranus and Neptune, were unlikely places to find life because their size had enabled them to retain hopelessly dense, deep and poisonous atmospheres. Even if they had the kind of surface you could stand on, you would be crushed by their gravity, and they would be far too cold to support any kind of life of the sort we know on Earth.

VENUS – FROM HEAVEN TO HELL

Enigmatic Venus, our nearest neighbour, seemed more hopeful. All we could see through telescopes was a brilliant, shining, featureless lamp in the heavens, cycling from disc to crescent and back again as it swung between us and the sun and we saw it lit from different angles. What mysteries might that tantalising veil conceal?

Svante Arrhenius

The fact that Venus is very similar in size to the Earth and nearer to the sun gave astronomers hope that underneath its dazzling veil of cloud there might lurk a green, tropical jungle. The Swedish chemist Svante Arrhenius (1859-1927), a winner of the Nobel Prize for Chemistry, speculated that the planet might be covered in swamps, much like the Earth of the Carboniferous period, and this idea was seized upon by a series of science fiction writers. In *Perelandra* (1943), the second of his 'Space Trilogy' novels, C S Lewis painted a beguiling portrait of Venus as a Garden of Eden in which floating islands of tropical vegetation drifted on a warm ocean under a golden ceiling of low cloud.

We were all in for a shock. The first interplanetary probes in the early 1960s soon established that Venus, far from being a tropical paradise, is the

Zark's Factoid...

The average surface temperature is 462 °C, and because Venus does not tilt on its axis, there is no seasonal variation.

most hellish planet in the solar system, hotter even than Mercury, with a surface temperature of more than 400 degrees Celsius and a mainly carbon dioxide atmosphere with a pressure 90 times that on Earth. Though it has been speculated that life could have got a foothold during Venus' younger, cooler days and that some form of microbial life could still cling on high in the atmosphere, Venus is clearly not the place to look for advanced life forms.

THE LURE OF MARS

For thousands of years, Mars has fascinated every human being who has had the intellectual curiosity to lift his head from the grind of daily life, gaze up at the heavens and wonder why certain 'stars' (the planets) trundle around the heavens on a regular cycle instead of staying in one place. The first telescopes revealed tantalising glimpses of surface features; river valleys? Mountains? Lakes? Cities? Even after Lowell's canals had been

NASA's Hubble Space Telescope snapped this picture of Mars on October 28 2005 within a day of its closest approach to Earth on the night of October 29.

dismissed as illusory, it was clear that Mars did have real features; smears, streaks and patches which looked as if they could be landforms such as canyons and promontories. It looked like a place you could walk on, perhaps even live on. It also, unmistakably, had ice caps, just like the Earth, and that meant water. Surely there ought to be life on Mars?

We humans seem to have been willing to seize on the slightest hope, as witness the reaction to the rather curious image of the 'face on Mars' captured by the Viking 1 orbiter in 1976. Certainly the mile-long rock in question in the Cydonia region looks

like a face – but then the willingness of the human brain to see faces in everything is well known, and given the number of irregular rocks lying on the surface of Mars it would be surprising if there was not at least one that looked a bit like a face. Needless to say, the resemblance only appears when the light is right, and a three-dimensional reconstruction makes it clear that the formation is entirely natural.

THE DISAPPOINTING TRUTH

By the time the 'face' in Cydonia was spotted, the NASA Mars missions had already put paid to dreams that Mars might be habitable by advanced beings. When the Mariner 4 probe performed a successful flyby on July 14 1965, the bitter truth was revealed. Mars is essentially a dry, dead world. Its many craters, like those on the moon, confirm not only that it is geologically moribund (there is no continental recycling through plate tectonics, as takes place on Earth) but that its lack of a substantial atmosphere has left it at the mercy of billions of years of bombardment by meteorites. Martian atmospheric pressure is less than one per cent of that on Earth, and there is virtually no oxygen. Mars is also in general much colder than Earth, thanks to the lack of an atmospheric cloak to insulate the planet and its distance from the sun (35 million miles further than the Earth). And the real killer – it has no permanent liquid water, at least not at the surface.

In the past forty-odd years, our knowledge of the surface of Mars has leapt from almost nil to enough to fill a thick (and copiously illustrated) *Rough Guide*. Here's what we now know about our second nearest planet:

- Mars is fundamentally constructed rather like Earth, with a metallic core and a rocky crust, but it is almost dead geologically compared to Earth, lacking continental drift and with very little volcanic activity.

- The loss of Mars' magnetosphere early in its history not only allowed the solar wind to strip the planet of its atmosphere but has exposed its surface to a constant lethal barrage of cosmic radiation.

- Mars now has an extremely thin atmosphere, barely one two-hundredth as dense as that of Earth, and what there is is mostly carbon dioxide.

- The thin atmosphere, along with its distance from the sun (half as far again as the Earth, on average) keeps average temperatures far below those on Earth, plummeting in places to -140 degrees Celsius or less.

- Mars is essentially a dry world. There is abundant evidence that many millions, probably billions, of years ago there were rivers, lakes and oceans, but all that has long gone, except for a few temporary traces of liquid water in certain conditions. The only substantial surface water is held within the ice caps; when these shrink during the Martian summer, the ice sublimates (evaporates straight from solid to gas) rather than forming liquid water.

A range of ingenious and so far inconclusive experiments by a series of landers over the past thirty-odd years has suggested that if there is life of any kind on Mars (still an unresolved question), it must be very simple or hiding far underground, most likely both.

So could there be life on Mars? And what form might it take?

One tentative clue that there could be life is the presence of methane, a gas which is well known to be generated by microbial action. Methane normally decays rapidly, so the fact the atmosphere contains any at all tells us that it is somehow being regenerated. While Mars' methane may well have a geological origin, it is possible that some undiscovered life form is responsible.

In 1984 a piece of direct evidence was found which seemed to indicate that life has existed on the Red Planet. Meteorite hunters in Antarctica (where the flat, icy surface makes meteorites much easier to spot than almost anywhere else on Earth) found a four-pound specimen which was identified (by its composition) as Martian. Inside ALH 84001 (as it was labelled), structures were found which look remarkably like microscopic creepy-crawlies, leading many to believe that they are organic fossils. Sadly there is now a strong consensus that this fascinating 'fossil' is not organic, although at the time the resemblance was enough to make President Bill Clinton make a special broadcast on the discovery.

A few small areas of the surface of Mars have now been mapped and photographed in great detail, showing us with extraordinary clarity just what you would see if you could stand (in a pressure suit of course) looking out over the pinky-brown landscape. Strewn with rocks and dusted with grit, it all looks rather like a building site, as if the developers had given the place up as a bad job several billion years ago and whizzed off to Earth to do their stuff there instead, without bothering to clear up behind them (sadly however, no abandoned diggers or pallets of bricks have so far been spotted).

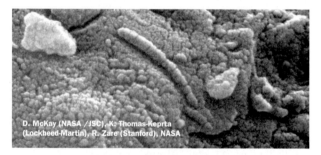
D. McKay (NASA /JSC), K. Thomas-Keprta (Lockheed-Martin), R. Zare (Stanford), NASA

What lies beneath the surface however, is completely unknown. Mars may lack the extensive cave systems of Earth, which have for the most part been formed by the action of our planet's abundant water on soft rock, but there are probably caverns, gorges, fissures and other underground spaces. If there is some form of life on Mars, these are surely the places to which it has retreated. In some dark, hollow region thousands of feet below ground, liquid water could persist all year round. There would be protection from cosmic radiation and a significantly denser atmosphere. It would also be a good deal warmer down there. So no one can yet rule out the possibility that there is life somewhere inside Mars – possibly even life you could see and touch, such as simple invertebrates. But until we find a way of exploring below the surface, we have no way of knowing for sure.

What created this unusual hole in Mars? The hole was discovered by chance in 2011 on images of the dusty slopes of Mars' Pavonis Mons volcano taken by the HiRISE instrument aboard the robotic Mars Reconnaissance Orbiter currently circling Mars. The hole appears to be an opening to an underground cavern, partly illuminated on the image left. Analysis of this and follow-up images revealed the opening to be about 35 meters across, while the interior shadow angle indicates that the underlying cavern is roughly 20 meters deep. Why there is a circular crater surrounding this hole remains a topic of speculation, as is the full extent of the underlying cavern. Holes such as this are of particular interest because their interior caves are relatively protected from the harsh surface of Mars, making them relatively good candidates to contain Martian life. These pits are therefore prime targets for possible future spacecraft, robots, and even human interplanetary explorers.

NASA, JPL, U. Arizona

Optimism that Mars might harbour simple life forms has grown with the realisation that simple, adapted organisms can survive in places on Earth which have traditionally been regarded as hopelessly inimical to life. These 'extremophiles', as they have been dubbed, have been found in places which are far too acidic, hot, cold or dense to support normal life forms, such as deep-sea hydrothermal vents, the hot springs of Yellowstone National Park and half a mile below the Antarctic ice.

Sol 3528
Before

Sol 3540
After

Mars Exploration Rover Mission, Cornell, JPL, NASA

What if a rock that looked like a jelly donut suddenly appeared on Mars? That's just what happened in front of the robotic Opportunity rover currently exploring the red planet. The unexpectedly placed rock, pictured above, was imaged recently by Opportunity after not appearing in other images taken as recently as twelve Martian days (sols) before. Given the intriguing mystery, the leading explanation is somewhat tame – the rock was recently scattered by one of the rover's tires. Even so, the rock's unusual light tones surrounding a red interior created interest in its composition – as well as causing it to be nicknamed Jelly Donut. A subsequent chemical analysis showed the rock has twice the abundance of manganese than any other rock yet examined – an unexpected clue that doesn't yet fit into humanity's understanding of the Martian geologic history. Opportunity, just passing its 10th anniversary on Mars, continues to explore the Murray Ridge section of the rim of 22-kilometer wide Endeavor Crater.

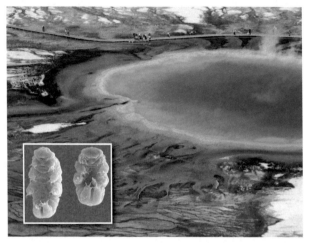

The world Famous Grand Prismatic Spring in Yellowstone National Park.
Inset: the tardigrade Hypsibius dujardini, imaged with a scanning electron microscope

Most of these organisms are invisible without a microscope, but there are notable exceptions, such as the Pompeii worm, a deep-sea worm which is happy at 80 degrees centigrade, and the tardigrades, tiny segmented creepy-crawlies. The tardigrades have it all – they can somehow survive a temperature range from below freezing to above the boiling point of water, pressures six times that of the deep ocean trenches, ionizing radiation which would kill any normal organism and even years of starvation. They can also go for decades without food or water. The extraordinary toughness of the tardigrade has even enabled it to survive in a test outside an orbiting space shuttle. Tardigrades are so durable partly because they can repair their own DNA and reduce their body water content to a few percent.

The appreciation the extremophiles have brought us of the limits of existence gives us hope that life of one kind or another, at least in simple form, could be more widespread than we thought. Mars may be a hostile place today, but it seems entirely likely that life got a hold there early on, when conditions were much more favourable.

"The bottom line is that if life ever got hold on Mars it probably still exists today" according to Dirk Schulze-Makuch (an astrobiology professor) and David Darling in their book *We Are Not Alone*. "There is plenty of evidence that the planet goes through intermittent warmer, wetter periods, probably associated with volcanic outbursts, when long-dormant microbes could reanimate, multiply and even evolve before the next big freeze sets in."

The European Space Agency's ExoMars mission, scheduled for launch in 2018, is intended to provide some answers by searching for organic molecules such as amino acids, the building blocks of proteins. If they are found, it will be fascinating to see whether the molecules are of left-handed construction (like those in all terrestrial organisms) or right-handed. If the former, it will suggest a common origin for life on Mars and Earth; if the latter, it will tell us that life on Mars has arisen independently. Either way it would be a fascinating discovery.

THE MOONS OF THE OUTER SOLAR SYSTEM

Although Jupiter, Saturn, Uranus and Neptune are almost certainly far too massive, cold and poisonous for life, their moons are rather more promising. Until the 1970s the four Galilean moons of Jupiter – the 'big four', Io, Europa, Ganymede and Callisto - were known only as bright beads of light performing an endless dance around the planet. The flybys by the Pioneer and Voyager missions and the observations from the orbiting probe Galileo have revealed that these moons are a treasure trove of surprises. We now know that at least three of Jupiter's moons and two of Saturn's have abundant water, and that despite the great distances of these bodies from the sun it appears that the water is at least partly in liquid form.

THE HIDDEN OCEAN OF EUROPA

Some of the strangest and most interesting predictions about the universe have come, by chance, from fictional writings. It was Jonathan Swift, in *Gulliver's Travels*, who predicted correctly that Mars had two undiscovered moons, and he wasn't too far out with their sizes and distances. In Arthur C Clarke's *2010: Odyssey Two* (1982) the hero is given the warning: "All these worlds are yours except Europa. Attempt no landings there". Clarke saw Europa, the second Galilean moon out from Jupiter at a distance of about 400,000 miles, as the most likely place to look for alien life in the solar system, and many modern scientists would agree with him.

In 1979 the Voyager 1 and Voyager 2 probes performed flybys which revealed that the pale blue surface of Europa was remarkably flat, but striated and criss-crossed with dark fault lines of some kind. The Galileo probe which arrived in 1995 and spent years studying Jupiter and its moons produced superb pictures of the surface of Europa, and we are still marvelling at them today.

Europa, Jupiter's moon, photographed by the American Galileo probe. (Credit: NASA/JPL)

Inside, Europa is built much like the Earth and Moon (it is slightly smaller than the Moon), with an iron core and a rocky mantle. Its surface, however, is composed almost entirely of ice, which forms a crust several miles thick. What excites scientists most about Europa is that between the rock and the ice there appears to be a hidden ocean of immense depth, containing perhaps three or four times as much water as all the oceans of the Earth.

How does all that water remain liquid on a world so far from the sun, with a surface temperature of something like -160˚ Celsius? The answer lies in the stresses and strains imposed on Europa by its gravitational relationship with Jupiter. Tidal flexing squeezes the whole satellite in tune with its three-and-a-half day orbit, heating up the interior through friction. Europa's ocean presumably has a temperature gradient which passes from freezing where it meets the bottom of the moon's icy shell down to something much warmer on the ocean bed many miles below.

The most recent observations suggest that Europa's oceans may be more active than we thought. There is new evidence that the ice shield behaves much as the Earth's crust does, with portions continually sliding apart and grinding together, which would account for the apparent leakage*. The fault lines and striations which mark the surface of Europa seem to be evidence of ocean upwellings which split the ice sheet open periodically, spreading mineral-stained water over the ice. If this so, parts of the ice may be relatively thin, measured in metres rather than miles.

*New Scientist 4.1.14

Images taken in 2012 by the Hubble Telescope have revealed plumes of water spouting into space from the moon's south pole. This raises the possibility of using an orbiter to scoop up the water for sampling – much easier than landing on the surface and drilling for it.

What sort of life could arise in such an environment? If the sea bed of Europa has the kind of activity we have found in the deep oceans of Earth, with deep-sea vents producing plumes of hot, mineral-rich water, it could be the cradle of simple microbial life, in the same way we think may have happened on Earth. Almost all life on Earth, including that in the oceans, depends on sunlight; in the sea, tiny organisms which live by photosynthesis gather energy and multiply, forming the foundation of a food chain which supports everything else. The new forms of life found in deep-sea hydrothermal vents, however, get their living from specialised bacteria which derive chemical energy from sulphur compounds. Is this happening on Europa? It seems quite possible. One specialist has examined the spectrum of light from the brown stains and found they are a close match with some terrestrial bacteria. Perhaps when we land a probe on Europa – now a rising priority in the space programme – we will be able to find evidence of life from surface deposits.

How far could life on this fascinating moon have evolved, over the billions of years of its existence?

Those who hope that the Europan seas will turn out to abound with creatures straight out of a sailor's nightmare may be a trifle optimistic. In the absence of sunlight (these waters must be totally without light) there is a limit to the available energy. A 2003 study hypothesised that creatures as large as shrimps might exist – which would still be a marvellous and fascinating discovery.

NASA artists' rendition of a space probe on one of Jupiter's satellites, Europa. The probe first penetrates the icy surface, then descends through the liquid ocean underneath to explore volcanoes or hydrothermal vents on the seafloor. Such probes could one day carry instruments based on the ESP.

Image: NASA/JPL

Zark's Factoid...
Europa is Jupiter's sixth satellite. Its orbital distance from Jupiter is 414,000 miles (670,900 km). It takes Europa three and a half days to orbit Jupiter. The same side of the Europa faces Jupiter at all times.

THE FOUNTAINS OF ENCELADUS

Enceladus was just one of the smaller moons of Saturn until the Cassini orbiter reported in 2005 that this little satellite has a liquid ocean which periodically shoots jets of water out into space as a result of tidal action. The water falls as showers of ice particles which have given the moon a brilliant white coating. The water contains carbon dioxide, methane and a variety of organic compounds, raising the tantalising possibility, as with Europa, that Enceladus could harbour life.

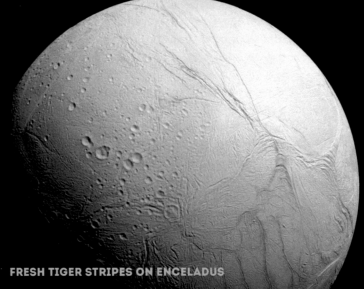

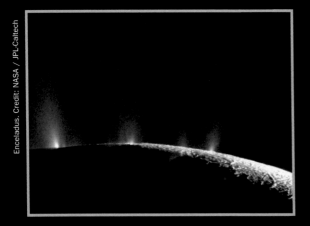

Enceladus. Credit: NASA / JPL-Caltech

FRESH TIGER STRIPES ON ENCELADUS

Pictured here is a high resolution Cassini image of Enceladus from a close flyby. Do underground oceans vent through the tiger stripes (in false-colour blue) on Saturn's moon Enceladus? The long features dubbed tiger stripes are known to spew ice from the moon's icy interior into space, creating a cloud of fine ice particles over the moon's south pole and creating Saturn's mysterious E-ring.

Cassini Imaging Team, SSI, JPL, ESA, NASA

TITAN – A DIFFERENT CHEMISTRY?

Saturn's largest moon, Titan, is the only moon apart from our own on which we have landed a space probe, and the only one in the solar system with a substantial atmosphere. Pictures relayed from the Huygens probe in 2005 show a landscape which is not so different from Earth's, with mountains, valleys and rivers. Unfortunately, although there is thought to be liquid water below the surface, the rivers are of methane and the temperature of -180° Celsius rules out 'life as we know it'.

Complex organic chemistry is undoubtedly going on on Titan however, and some form of life cannot be ruled out. The Titanians would have to breathe molecular hydrogen, metabolize it with acetylene and exhale methane instead of carbon dioxide, but there is nothing in the rules of chemistry to say this could not work.

What of the rest of the outer planets and their moons? Most of them have water – Triton, Neptune's only sizeable moon, is largely composed of it – but it is frozen. There is little if any permanent liquid water to be found beyond Jupiter, and no realistic chance of life. It looks as if we will have to go a little further than the solar system to find the kind of aliens we can talk to.

This artist's concept shows a possible scenario for the internal structure of Titan, as suggested by data from NASA's Cassini spacecraft. Scientists have been trying to determine what is under Titan's organic-rich atmosphere and icy crust. Data from the radio science experiment make the strongest case yet for a global subsurface ocean, sitting above a subsurface layer of high-pressure ice and a water-infused silicate core.

Image: A. Tavani

This mosaic of three frames provides unprecedented detail of the high ridge area including the flow down into a major river channel from different sources.

Image: NASA/JPL

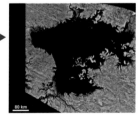

Ligeia Mare, shown here in an artistically enhanced image from NASA's Cassini mission, is the second largest known body of liquid on Saturn's moon Titan. It is filled with liquid hydrocarbons, such as ethane and methane, and is one of the many seas and lakes that bejewel Titan's north polar region.

Image: NASA/JPL-Caltech/ASI/Cornell

80 km

4

HOW TO BUILD AN ALIEN

"IF WE EVER SUCCEED IN
COMMUNICATING WITH
CONCEPTUALISING BEINGS IN OUTER
SPACE, THEY WON'T BE SPHERES,
PYRAMIDS, CUBES OR PANCAKES.
IN ALL PROBABILITY THEY WILL LOOK
AN AWFUL LOT LIKE US"

ROBERT BIERI, SCIENTIST

Many and varied are the forms in which alien life has been imagined by the science fiction writers. Tiny beetle-like organisms, mistaken by a gardener for pests (Robert Sheckley); jellyfish-like monsters of the deep, shielded by metallic armour (John Wyndham); an interstellar cloud of hydrogen, settling around a star every few thousand years to recharge its batteries (Fred Hoyle); and all manner of creatures loosely based on insects, lizards, apes, birds or plants – to say nothing of robots in all shapes and sizes.

Of course, the majority of aliens depicted in TV and film dramas (until very recently at least) have been remarkably similar in body plan to humans, which is unsurprising given that they have to be played by human actors. The advent of 3D computer graphics and digitally-created digital aliens has freed the more recent films from this restriction and given us some marvellous visions of how an alien might look. So how are they likely to look?

J B S Haldane

WHY BIOLOGY MAY BE UNIVERSAL

The great biologist J B S Haldane famously remarked, "The universe is not only queerer than we suppose, it is queerer than we can suppose". Many scientists and writers have championed this view, imagining life forms which look nothing like anything seen on Earth. Surely, the day we meet an alien creature, it will come as a terrible shock. Surely it will look like nothing we could have imagined in our worst nightmares – cubes, blobs, glowing clouds, creeping tides of jelly?

In fact there are good reasons for believing that biology is likely to work in more or less the same way pretty much everywhere we go in the universe. Biology is based on chemistry, and we have ample evidence that the chemistry we know is universal. The stars, dust clouds, planets and other coalescences of matter that make up the visible material of the universe are built almost entirely of the two

Zark's Factoid...

Aliens would be "just like humans," not only in appearance and biology but in weaknesses, such as "greed, violence and a tendency to exploit others' resources."
Simon Conway Morris, professor of evolutionary paleobiology at Cambridge University

lightest and simplest elements, hydrogen and helium, with all the other elements having been generated (in much tinier quantities) by a process called nucleosynthesis within stars. Wherever we look we see the same elements and compounds, connected by the same chemistry.

THE MAGIC OF CARBON

One of these elements is overwhelmingly important to life, in fact it's probably indispensable to it – carbon, the fourth most abundant element in the universe after hydrogen, helium and oxygen. This is because the carbon atom has a structure which puts it head and shoulders above all other elements when it comes to combining with other atoms to form molecules. Its insatiable appetite for electrons belonging to other atoms makes it by far the most promiscuous of all the elements.

Much has been made by sci-fi writers of the element silicon as an alternative basis for life. It is true that silicon, which sits right next to carbon in the periodic table and is the only element that comes close in terms of the versatility of its bonding, shares many of its properties. However there are some killer differences. Like carbon, silicon loves bonding with oxygen, but the result, silicon dioxide or silica (SiO2) is a solid, which makes it virtually impossible for a body to absorb it. It doesn't even dissolve in water. It is highly unlikely that on a planet equipped with both elements (which most planets probably are), life would take the silicon route (it certainly didn't on Earth, although we have vastly more silicon here than carbon). Life, let alone complex life, is quite difficult enough to make with carbon; with silicon it may well be impossible.

So given that carbon is THE element, everywhere in the universe, for the building of life, how does the process begin? If we know that, we will know whether it is likely to be happening elsewhere.

Carbon's affinity for pretty much every other element it comes across allows it to form an uncountable array of compounds with an almost equally uncountable range of

Zark's Factoid...

Carbon forms the key component for all known naturally occurring life on Earth. It was named as an element by Antoine Lavoisier in 1789.

carbon

6

C

12.011

Life on our planet is thought to have arisen out of a pond-scum-like mix of chemicals. Some of these chemicals are thought to have come from a planet-forming disk of gas and dust that swirled around our young sun. Meteorites carrying the chemicals might have crash-landed on Earth.

properties, from CO2 (carbon dioxide) to molecules which have names hundreds of letters long and formulae which look like accidents in a Scrabble factory. Some of these compounds are the precursors to life; we are all built of them.

THE PUZZLE OF LIFE'S ORIGIN

So how do you get from fancy carbon molecules to life? The answer is – with great difficulty.

Despite decades of theorising and experimenting, we still do not know just how a bunch of carbon molecules ever managed to get together to form increasingly complex organic molecules and eventually, self-replicating organisms - life. What we do know is that after a few hundred million years of extreme heat and violence, during which the hot young Earth was bombarded with comets, meteorites and other debris of the young solar system, it gradually settled down, and that pretty much as soon as the fireworks had stopped, primitive life appeared.

The key prerequisite to the birth of life was of course water. Everything we know about life tells us that it cannot exist without it. All plants and animals are composed largely of water, and life almost certainly evolved in it.

Chemicals cannot dissolve and react with one another without a solvent, and water is the universe's favourite solvent. It has other remarkable properties which have contributed to the development of the organic molecules which are the precursors of life, such as:

- It is exceptionally transparent, which has the benefit to life of allowing light through it.

- The unusual molecular structure of water makes its molecules highly attractive to one another, which is responsible for water's peculiar surface tension, essential to many aquatic invertebrates. The same property makes possible capillary action, without which plants could not draw water up into their cells. Without this property, there would be no vascular plants (flowers, trees, grass etc).

- Water has a high specific heat, meaning it takes a lot of energy to heat it up, so it heats and cools very slowly. This same property means it can retain vast quantities of warmth for long periods, acting as a heat reservoir during winter or extended cold periods. Conversely it keeps the environment cool in hot conditions.

- The strange fact that water is less dense as a solid than as a liquid means that ice floats. Without this oceans would freeze from the bottom up, so ice ages would be likely to kill everything off.

THE DNA MOLECULE

The formula for life is extremely complicated. To simplify greatly, all known life is built on DNA (deoxyribonucleic acid), a spectacularly complex molecule which is one of a group of nucleic acids. DNA is preceded by the slightly simpler RNA (a similar molecule built in a single strand instead of two). Nucleic acids are very large molecules built principally of nucleotides, sugars and phosphates. DNA replicates with the assistance of proteins, another group of enormously complex compounds which are built from amino acids.

I'm Alive!

All life is built on the same 20 amino acids, out of a possible range of many thousands. The chances are that different ones will have been used where life has originated elsewhere, although some of the simpler ones have been found to form quite readily in the right conditions, so we may well encounter at least some of the same amino acids wherever life occurs.

Only five elements are involved in all this - hydrogen, oxygen, nitrogen, carbon and phosphorus - but rather a lot of

them are needed to make one of the building blocks of life. It has been estimated that there are something like two hundred billion atoms in a single DNA molecule. Putting all this show together in the lab has proved hopelessly beyond us so far, even with the marvellously sophisticated technology of the 21st century. We have got as far as amino acids, but that's about it. It must have been a challenge for nature too, but that didn't stop DNA, and simple life, appearing somehow very early in the Earth's history. Once the initial violent bombardment had stopped and the dust had settled on our young planet, single-celled organisms appeared pretty much straight away, as evidenced by the fossil record.

LIFE FROM SPACE?

For many years life was thought to have been sparked off through some form of chemical synthesis in a 'warm little pond' somewhere (to use Charles Darwin's phrase). A more recent

Charles Darwin

suggestion is that the deep-sea vents mentioned in the last chapter could have been the cradle of life. Now we are not so sure that life was first built on Earth at all. There are those who hypothesise that it came to us from space, which would explain how it got going on a planet which at the time was apparently hostile to life, with a reducing carbon dioxide-dominated atmosphere.

The term 'panspermia' (universal seeding) was coined by the ancient Greeks. Now, after languishing as a fringe idea until recent times, it is suddenly being taken quite seriously, following the realisation that organic molecules of surprising complexity are found in space.

We have known for many years that there is organic chemistry going on out in the void, but we have only recently appreciated how much. A meteorite which fell in Australia in 1969 was found to contain amino acids and peptides, telling us that these highly complex molecules must have been whizzing around in space for billions of years. In 2008 a compound called aminoacetonitrile was detected in Sagittarius B2, an interstellar gas cloud 400 light years away. This is one step away from the amino acid glycine. And then in 2009 glycine itself was found, on the surface of a comet, 81P/Wild 2. It is only one further step (though a tricky one) from amino acids to protein, which replicates DNA. In 2013 ethanimine, a precursor of one of the bases of DNA, was found in Sagittarius B2. All this despite the fact that these complex molecules are immensely difficult to spot compared with the elements and simple compounds which make up most of the universe.

It seems that the chemistry we see in the lab down here on Earth happens in space too – just very, very slowly, because it's so cold out there. But time is one thing the universe has in plenty.

WANDERING ROCKS

We already know that our own planets can swap material, from the number of Martian meteorites we have found on Earth. But how could the key ingredients of life possibly get sent from one part of the galaxy to another?

They may come with the package, as it were, having been formed along with the protoplanetary disc which condensed to form the sun and planets. But they could be seeded from star to star. We know from our observations of the solar system that gravitational forces between planets, asteroids, comets

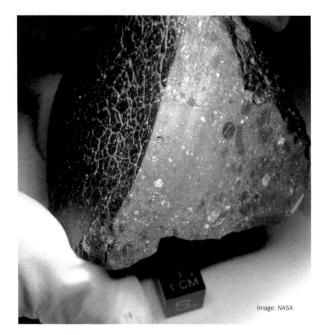

Image: NASA

NASA-funded researchers analyzing a small meteorite that may be the first discovered from the Martian surface or crust have found it contains 10 times more water than other Martian meteorites from unknown origins.

This new class of meteorite was found in 2011 in the Sahara Desert. Designated Northwest Africa (NWA) 7034, and nicknamed "Black Beauty," it weighs approximately 11 ounces (320 grams). After more than a year of intensive study, a team of U.S. scientists determined the meteorite formed 2.1 billion years ago during the beginning of the most recent geologic period on Mars, known as the Amazonian.

and moons can occasionally flip one of these bodies out of its orbit and send it whizzing off into interstellar space. The random close approach of two stars will send both solar systems into chaos (see chapter 6).

It's a little-realised fact that space is full of cold, dark and lonely lumps of rock and ice which once belonged to solar systems but have been cast into the outer darkness by the fickle finger of fate. It's thought that the galaxy could contain billions of lost planets and countless trillions of smaller chunks of rock and ice. 'Full' of course is a relative term, space being rather large. (The fact that the orbits of all the planets are so circular suggests that we have been lucky – no other star can have come closer to the Sun than ten billion miles or so since the solar system formed.)

Bodies in the region of the orbit of Jupiter are travelling around the sun at about 13 km per second (40,000 km per hour). If one of them got tiddlywinked out of the solar system at the same speed (close to that of one of the current space probes) it could be passing the nearest star within 100,000 years, and if it had set out when the solar system was young it would be well out of the Milky Way by now. If it was a planet-sized body with water and enough internal heat to stay warm, it could conceivably even have sustained any simple life forms it started out with, as well as the building blocks.

The speed with which primitive life in the form of the first single-celled organisms (the Archaea and the Bacteria) appeared on Earth suggests that it is likely to crop up wherever the right conditions arise. However one key feature of life on Earth tells us it can't be as easy as that; all known life is based on the same molecule, DNA, and all DNA molecules show the same 'chirality', that is they are all twisted the same way – to the left. The fact that all the DNA we find is built from effectively the same molecule is strong evidence that life here arose once and once only.

THE THREE BILLION YEAR WAIT FOR ANIMALS

So if life was in such a hurry to get cracking on Earth as soon as things cooled down enough, it must have started evolving pretty quickly, right? Wrong.

For around three billion years, the primeval slime stayed just as it was – slime. It wasn't until about seven or eight hundred million years ago (no one is sure exactly when) that the first very

Zark's Factoid...
Exactly when the first life on Earth - the ancestors of modern bacteria - began is a subject of debate, but evidence suggests it could be as much as 4 billion years ago.

simple animals appeared – tiny, primitive worms which have left no clear fossils.

Simple as they were, the worms were a crucial step forward. They were only possible because there had been one rather important change to some of the slime. Some two billion years after life's first appearance, a new, more interesting kind of slime had appeared, built of cells called eukaryotes.

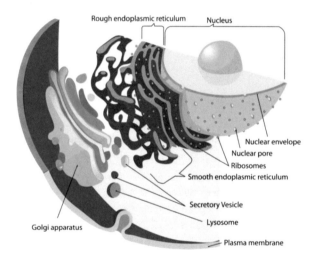

The diagram shows a endomembrane system on a Eukaryote cell.

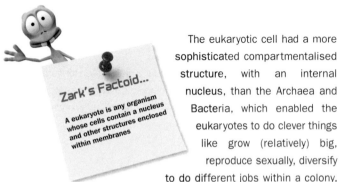

Zark's Factoid...

A eukaryote is any organism whose cells contain a nucleus and other structures enclosed within membranes

The eukaryotic cell had a more sophisticated compartmentalised structure, with an internal nucleus, than the Archaea and Bacteria, which enabled the eukaryotes to do clever things like grow (relatively) big, reproduce sexually, diversify to do different jobs within a colony, and eat other cells. It was some of the eukaryotes which evolved into those first tiny worms. In fact they went on to give rise to all the visible forms of life on Earth today, from mushrooms to merchant bankers. The eukaryotes are still around us – they are us. We are built of eukaryotic cells.

The emergence of the eukaryotes is presumed to have taken so long because the slow, millimetre-by-millimetre process of evolution needed all that time before it threw up all the complex parts and faculties of the eukaryotic body – like a rowing boat evolving, blind step by blind step, into an ocean liner.

Meanwhile the Archaea and the Bacteria continued to stick with the 'simple is best' strategy and are pretty much the same today - they just have more species. In fact they pervade every medium that can support life.

Zark's Factoid...

Photosynthesis is a process used by plants and other organisms to convert light energy, normally from the sun, into chemical energy that can be later released to fuel the organisms' activities.

LIFE GETS TO BREATHE AT LAST

In the course of photosynthesis, the early life forms pumped out oxygen, an element which was rare on the early Earth – if you tried to land on the Earth of three billion years ago you would have quickly stifled to death without a space suit. Gradually the amount of oxygen in the air built up, until about 2.4 billion years ago, when our planet was about half its present age, the process had transformed the hostile atmosphere into the oxygen-rich air we breathe today, which opened the way for organisms to adopt a new, more efficient metabolism. In doing so, they at last created a world in which complex animals could live. This, along with the rise of the eukaryotes, set the scene for a dramatic change.

THE CAMBRIAN EXPLOSION

Around 570 million years ago, life on Earth underwent a period of unprecedentedly rapid change called the Cambrian Explosion. From a world which contained no animals, no creepy-crawlies, no proper plants, no visible life at all except for various kinds of living goo, the fossil record shows that the oceans were suddenly awash with strange beasts, from worms

Zark's Factoid...
The Cambrian explosion was the relatively rapid appearance, around 570 million years ago, of most major animal phyla, as demonstrated in the fossil record. This was accompanied by major diversification of other organisms

and jellyfish to creatures closely resembling giant shrimps and fish. After that, life never looked back. The process of evolution had shot into top gear.

Just to clarify briefly how the process of evolution works: thanks to random genetic mutation, every generation throws up creatures which are very slightly different from one another and from their parents. Individuals which have some tiny advantage – being able to digest food a little faster, for example, or move faster or breed at a lower temperature – will survive and reproduce a little better, passing their modifications on to a disproportionately large share of the next generation. In this way, step by step, complexity is blindly built on complexity. As time passes, ten kinds of creature become a thousand and a thousand become a million, ranging from the very simple to the extremely complicated. Since life first began, these minute changes have brought one particular branch of life all the way from the primeval slime to creatures which can read and write books about aliens. And merchant bankers.

Which takes us back to the point - what does all this have to do with alien life? Simple - if we understand how life has developed on Earth, we have a better idea how – and if - it is likely to develop on other planets.

So would life follow a similar path on another planet?

HOW TO BUILD A WORKING ANIMAL

In the next chapter we'll look at Earth and its place in the universe and see what the chances are of finding another planet that could also be a cradle of advanced life. But assuming Earth-like conditions can be found elsewhere, would life turn out the same way? What's to stop beings on other worlds turning out to look like slugs, tortoises or trees – or like nothing we have ever imagined?

We have already seen that life, wherever it is found in the universe, is overwhelmingly likely to be based on carbon compounds and dependent on water. We have seen that after hundreds of millions of years of random chemical activity, all life on Earth appears to have originated in one lucky throw of the dice – the enormously complex chain of chemical events which led to the construction of the first DNA molecule.

The Human Blueprint

The fact that life did arise on Earth, and that it did so pretty much as soon as it could, suggests that it would happen again on any planet where the conditions were right. But what it would it look like?

If you are one of those who embrace the notion that life elsewhere is sure to turn out to be impossibly strange, there may be good reason to think again. Of all the millions of ways life could evolve once it has got started, it may be that only a very few would ever be viable. That's because life, wherever it arises, has certain basic imperatives – it must feed, move, grow, survive and reproduce. The forces of evolution will make sure that animals that don't do these things well will quickly disappear. The fantasy aliens of Doctor Who and much early science fiction simply wouldn't work, just as a bicycle with square wheels wouldn't work.

THE REQUIREMENTS OF SURVIVAL

First, any animal is going to require a purpose-built **body** which enables it to get around efficiently, finding and pursuing food or sexual partners and negotiating its habitat without excessive damage or wear. The body has to be big enough to house a decent brain, stomach, heart and so on, yet not so big that gravity is going to make movement difficult. The optimum size range for animals will be larger on smaller planets with lower gravity and smaller on bigger planets with high gravity, but there are good reasons to think life-bearing planets will resemble the Earth in size, as we'll see in the last chapter, so advanced creatures are not likely to be very much bigger or smaller than ourselves.

Unless a body is very small, it will need some form of **skeleton** (either an internal one, as in the vertebrates, or an external one, as in crabs and other crustaceans).

It will need some means of propulsion, which is usually going to mean **limbs** – on land, that means at least two flexible,

jointed, muscular extensions with something at the end to run, grip or stand with, while in water it will mean fins, and in air it will mean wings. If two of those limbs evolve into grasping appendages – hands, which are a lot more useful in pairs – the animal is going to have to learn to run on the other limbs – legs, with feet at the end.

Every organism's body needs a protective **skin** or armour, hide or carapace to protect its organs, smooth its passage through its environment (whether water, earth, vegetation or whatever) and keep it from drying out or getting waterlogged.

The animal will need built-in **tools** or **weapons** to enable it to procure food, whether animal or vegetable, and reduce it to a digestible form. That means something like teeth, claws or limbs designed for crushing or binding.

There'll be a **digestive system** to enable it to convert the food into a form it can use for fuel and to build and repair its body, and of course a **reproductive system**, which can be kept safely tucked away when not in use (the appearance of two sexes, for complex reasons, is one of the key features of the success of animal life on Earth).

Another essential is appropriate **protection** against predators, which may range from cryptic colouring to spikes, a horny shield or the ability to jump, swim, fly or run fast.

Every animal will need a range of well-tuned senses to tell it what's going on around it – and there are only so many kinds of **senses**. Touch/feel, smell/taste, hearing and sight pretty much cover it, along with certain more subtle senses, such as the ability of some birds to navigate by sensing the Earth's magnetic field, and the lateral lines of fishes, which detect vibrations transmitted through water.

A LOOK AT VISION

Let's take a look at sight for a moment. Eyes have evolved independently on Earth many times since the rise of animal life in the Cambrian period over 500 million years ago. We know from the way the human eye works that it evolved separately from, for example, the design used by the squids and octopi, even though they look superficially similar. It seems highly probably that vision would evolve repeatedly on any planet, and that the camera eye adopted by humans, as the most effective naturally-evolved design we know, is the best choice and hence the solution associated with the most intelligent and dominant species.

How many eyes? Earth's creatures have evolved various numbers and arrangements, but all advanced animals on Earth – the vertebrates - have long since rationalised this down to two, which allows either an emphasis on binocular vision (for hunting) or all-round vision (for avoiding predators). Clearly two must be the optimum number for survival, or nature wouldn't have universally chosen it.

And where would they be positioned? Surely at the top or

front of the animal, just as they are on terrestrial animals – on the **head**.

Hearing will be performed by **ears**, which are likely to protrude from the head and be dished in shape to allow efficient sound gathering. There will again probably be two, to enable the direction of sounds to be determined.

The head is also the obvious place for the mouth and teeth.

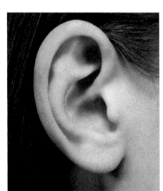

Operating the body and processing the input from the senses is going to need a brain, and the need for lightning communication between eyes and **brain** suggests that the head is also the best place for the latter.

BILATERAL SYMMETRY

Most organisms are designed to maintain progress in a particular direction, with the eyes and ears at the front to see what's coming up, along with the mouth and teeth to deal with it. That's why a head develops. This means the front is different from the back, and the top (facing the sky and perhaps needing to be camouflaged or protected) is different from the bottom (interacting with the ground). The sides, however, can be identical. Hence the bilateral symmetry which is almost universal among animals, and the pairing of tools and organs. The same logic is likely to apply to creatures on other worlds.

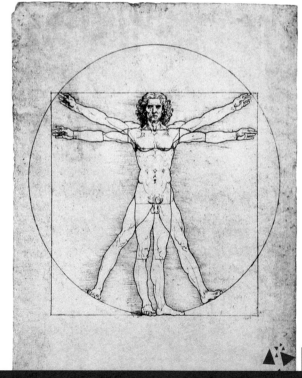

IS INTELLIGENCE INEVITABLE?

There is a widespread assumption that intelligent beings like us are in some sense the ultimate aim of life; the destiny and direction of all living things. To us, intelligence is so obviously desirable that we find it difficult to look at the world in any other way. We see ourselves as the victors in some kind of race from slime to intellectual brilliance.

In fact of course, humans are simply one of countless solutions which life on Earth has come up with to the problem of how to survive and prosper. The actual motive force of life is the gene itself, as was first properly explained by Professor Richard Dawkins, who long before he became famous for debunking religion wrote a marvellous book called

Richard Dawkins

The Selfish Gene (1976). Genes propagate by building ever-better bodies. The bodies themselves are discarded if unfit for purpose, or improved to make them more so – the genes don't care, they just 'want' to make more genes.

This insight enables us to realise that intelligence is only important to humans because it's given us our personal path to dominance. Elephants could argue that success in life is all about trunks (or sheer bulk), while birds could look down (literally) on the rest of the natural world and scorn it for having failed to learn to fly. If intelligence were some kind of end goal to which all organisms aspire, why didn't the dinosaurs evolve more of it? They had plenty of time, as Paul Davies points out in The Eerie Silence (2010).

A life-rich distant planet which does not happen to contain creatures who can read, write and study the stars should not therefore be looked upon as some kind of tragic failure. It's quite possible that planets where animal life ever evolves intelligence are rare – perhaps fabulously rare. It may be that we could survey a thousand planets where life has been developing and diversifying for billions of years (like ours) without finding any sign of the high IQs we value so much. Another reason for doubting that technology is going to be easy to find in the universe.

SIMILAR PROBLEMS, SIMILAR SOLUTIONS

For the practical reasons explained above, animals on a far-off planet may not look all that different from those on Earth. If one day we do discover a planet bearing advanced life forms, its oceans, deserts, jungles, ice caps and swamps are likely to be peopled by organisms which have adapted to those environments in much the same ways life has here. The oceans will have fish-like creatures which prey on smaller fish-like creatures and are in turn preyed on by bigger ones which will probably be built for speed and power and have large dagger-shaped teeth – just like sharks. Vegetated areas of land will have populations of large creatures which have evolved to digest plants, and these will be hunted by fast, powerful animals with big teeth – very much like big cats, hyenas or wolves. Small animals will use teeth and claws to prey on smaller creatures, and the smallest animals will rely on plant life.

One of the most realistic portrayals of life on another planet to date was rendered in the 2009 James Cameron film Avatar, in which (apart from an improbable number of huge dinosaur-

like carnivores and the famous hanging mountains) thought had been given to designing life forms which would actually work. Computer-generated imagery helped them to resemble aliens we could believe in.

GROWING ALIKE, NOT APART

Hummingbird Hawkmoth (Macroglossum stellatarum) and verbena flowers

One very strong piece of evidence for the idea that life is not infinitely variable is a phenomenon biologists call convergence. Sometimes two unrelated animals or plants, instead of becoming less similar as they evolve, actually start to look more and more like one another, because they are pursuing the same 'trades'.

For example, it's pretty easy to tell a moth from a bird, until you look at the European hummingbird hawk moth. This little insect, found across much of Europe, North Africa and Asia, hovers in front of nectar-bearing flowers in exactly the same way as the bird after which it was named. Like the bird, it has evolved short, very fast-moving wings and an unusually long proboscis to enable it to hover in the same position while drawing nectar from flowers whose calyxes are too long for most insects.

Other examples of convergence appear in the similarities between conventional (placental) mammals and the marsupials of the Antipodes, and in desert plants from Mexico and Africa which have evolved almost exactly similar structures to preserve their moisture.

All this suggests that organisms may not evolve in startling and unimaginable ways after all. They will develop to suit their environment, and everywhere in the universe, the range of environments where life does well is likely to be similar – based primarily on liquid water, a rocky crust and an oxygen-rich atmosphere. So alien creatures may well look superficially rather like the animals we know here on Earth.

If we are lucky enough one day to meet another intelligent species, it is likely to be built on similar principles – though of course the end result may be rather different. Something like a head with two recognisable eyes and ears seems likely, and a longish body with paired limbs of some kind. They are likely to communicate with sound, which means some form of speech. They will probably have to adorn and protect themselves with some kind of clothing. Beyond that, we can only speculate.

WHY ARE HUMANS TOP?

So why has one particular group of animals become the dominant species; the most complex, successful (by any realistic measure) and powerful of all the countless millions of animals which have evolved on Earth?

Some argue that it is just our own vanity that has convinced us that we are the most successful species, but just look at how many of us there are. The rest of the animal kingdom follows the 'bigger means fewer'

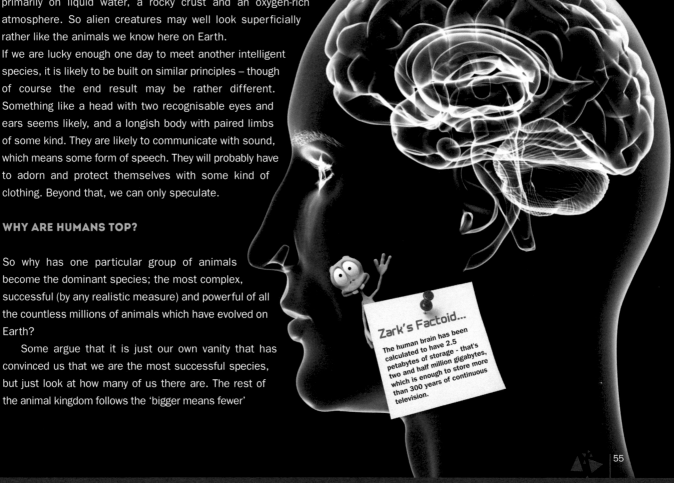

Zark's Factoid...

The human brain has been calculated to have 2.5 petabytes of storage - that's two and half million gigabytes, which is enough to store more than 300 years of continuous television.

– ie there are more mice in the world than deer and more deer than whales. On this scale, there are ten thousand times more humans than there ought to be.

In truth evolution is blind. It has no end, no destination, no 'up'. It is only from our perspective that we look upon the development of humans as a long selection process, with the losers whittled out at every stage and a range of winners going through to the next round. Yes, from our point of view we have leapt many hurdles and squeezed through many bottlenecks on our way to winning nature's lottery by becoming Top Species. But then if we hadn't, we wouldn't be here to pat ourselves on the back.

We have had a great deal of luck, but we still wouldn't have made it if we had not had the physical assets that make us what we are – most important of all, a highly-developed brain, which essentially evolved because we became, millions of years ago, an exceptionally social species. Interaction with our fellows, with all the cooperation, competition, manipulation and deceit that involves, has made us the brainboxes we are today. On other planets too, it is likely that intelligence will go hand in hand with a highly-organised society, as well as technology. Intelligent creatures are not likely to fly solo.

THE FUTURE OF INTELLIGENCE

Of course, *Homo sapiens* does not represent an end point in evolution – simply the stage we happen to have reached now. What might become of intelligent bipeds like us in the future?

Many thousands of years from now, if we are still here, it is possible that our technology will have freed us from the need to hunt, fight, run, taste and smell, or cope with injury, illness, even death – though immortality could be a problem, if we wish to make room for our offspring. We could be sitting inside machines, like the Daleks or the Mekon in the Dan Dare cartoon strip, managing our environment through automated machinery. But would we want to? Wouldn't we want to hang on to the pleasures of the body – eating, exploring, sport, sex? Wouldn't we arrange things so that we could combine the benefits of technology with the pleasures of being human? That's certainly what we lucky, leisured humans of the developed world are trying to do now.

Without a time machine, we have no way of knowing how future generations of humanity are going to tackle this one. Perhaps if we ever do manage to make contact with another civilisation, one that's a few thousand years more advanced than we are, we'll learn the answer.

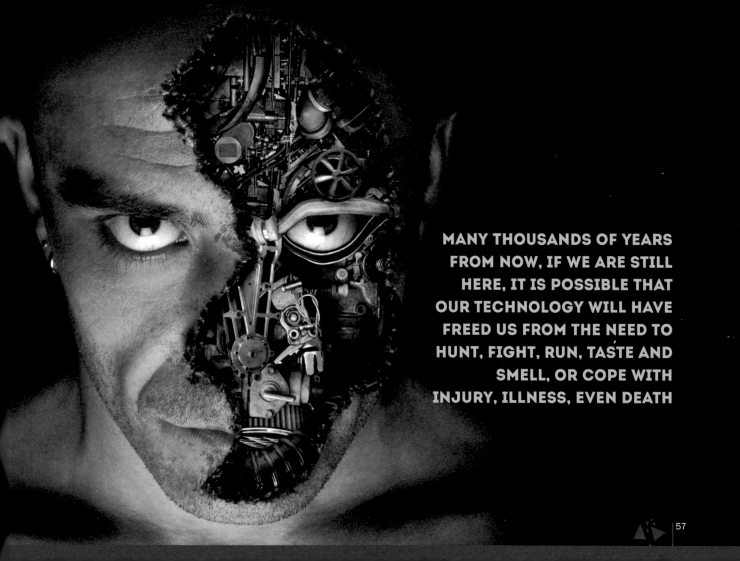

MANY THOUSANDS OF YEARS FROM NOW, IF WE ARE STILL HERE, IT IS POSSIBLE THAT OUR TECHNOLOGY WILL HAVE FREED US FROM THE NEED TO HUNT, FIGHT, RUN, TASTE AND SMELL, OR COPE WITH INJURY, ILLNESS, EVEN DEATH

5 REACHING FOR THE STARS

"IN RECENT YEARS WE HAVE DISCOVERED THAT... THERE ARE MORE PLANETS IN THE UNIVERSE THAN THERE ARE SAND GRAINS ON ALL THE BEACHES OF ALL THE COASTLINES OF ALL THE CONTINENTS"

MARCUS CHOWN, NEW SCIENTIST

To find the interesting aliens, the kind we could play chess with or talk to about quantum physics, we are going to have go to the stars. We started off with a discussion of the Drake Equation, a means of estimating how many alien civilisations there might be out there for us to communicate with. Things have moved on a bit since the equation was first formulated, as we have a much deeper understanding of the factors that control the incidence of life, and particularly advanced life, in the universe.

PLANETS BY THE BUCKETFUL

Let's begin with the good news – there are lots and lots of stars out there, and we now know that there are even more planets. A 2010 study estimated that the observable universe contains 300 sextillion (3×10^{23}) stars – that's 300,000 million million million. And that's just the observable universe,* which occupies a sphere with a diameter of around 90 billion light years. The actual universe must be bigger, though we have no way of knowing how much bigger. It could be a million times as big, an octillion times as big, or infinite.

*NOTE: The observable universe is the region from which light has had time to reach us since it all started with the Big Bang 13.8 billion years ago. Light has only actually travelled 13.8 billion light years since, so nothing further away will ever be visible, but the universe has been expanding in the meantime, so the galaxies we see 13 billion light years away are in reality three times further away by now.

Until quite recently we didn't know whether any other stars had planets; perhaps the solar system was a freak, the planets created (as astronomers once believed) through a chance encounter between the Sun and another star, an extremely rare cosmic event. Now we know that most stars have a retinue of planets - perhaps virtually all of them.

The first planet-hunting was done by looking for stars that wobbled. If a star can be seen to be rotating with a slight rhythmic waggle (using measurements of the Doppler shift, which tell us if one side is advancing (rotating towards us) while the other is retreating), this shows that there is another massive body orbiting it and pulling upon it, either an invisibly dim companion star or a large planet. Exactly the same thing happens with the Sun and Jupiter, though as Jupiter is less than one thousandth of the Sun's mass, their common centre of gravity is actually inside the Sun.

KEPLER – THE PLANET HUNTER

The first few planets discovered were therefore giant ones like Jupiter, many of them orbiting much closer to their stars than Jupiter does (partly a function of the way the search works of course – a close planet orbits faster, so it transits its star more often). Such planets are not likely to be homes for life (though their satellites could be, as we saw in chapter 3). The search went up several gears in 2009, when NASA launched Kepler, a spacecraft which is devoted solely to the search for other planets. Kepler is now trailing the Earth in orbit around the Sun, gradually falling further away from us to minimise interference. Its light sensors are pointing out of the plane of the solar system (partly to avoid the risk of their being blinded by the Sun) in the direction of our journey around the galaxy, so Kepler is looking towards other stars which are in the same region of the galaxy as we are and therefore likely to be within the galactic habitable zone (explained in chapter 6).

Kepler works by looking for tiny periodic dips in the light of an individual star caused by a planet passing in front of it. For

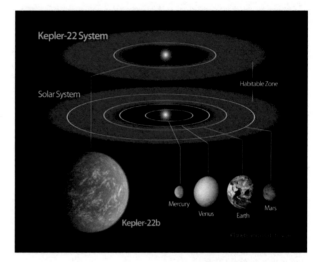

example, a planet like Earth passing in front of a star like the Sun would, seen from a distance, reduce the star's brightness by a factor of about one part in 12,000 for the 13 hours of the transit (we can see the same thing happening from Earth when Venus or Mercury passes in front of the Sun). If Kepler sees the same dip repeated every so often at intervals of weeks, months or years, we know it has observed a planet. From the period we know how far it is from its star, and from the dip in brightness we know how big it is.

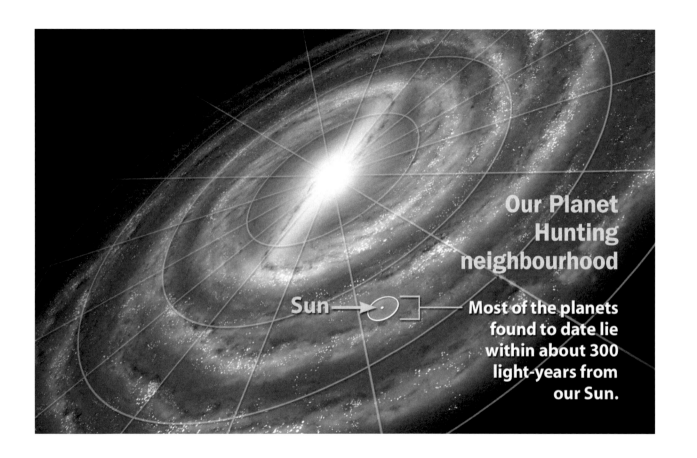

Our Planet Hunting neighbourhood

Sun →

Most of the planets found to date lie within about 300 light-years from our Sun.

Although it looks like fiction, this artist's vision of sunset on an alien world is based on fact – the recent discovery of a hot, jupiter-sized planet orbiting in triple star system HD 188753. Only 149 light-years away in the constellation Cygnus, HD 188753's massive planet was detected by astronomer Maciej Konacki after analyzing detailed spectroscopic data from the Keck Observatory. The large planet itself is depicted at the upper left in this imagined view from the well-illuminated surface of a hypothetical rocky moon. From this perspective, the closest, hottest and most massive star in the triple system, a star only a little hotter than the Sun, has set below distant peaks. The two other suns nearing the horizon are both cooler and farther from the large planet. While other hot, jupiter-like planets are known to orbit nearby stars, the "crowded" multiple star nature of this system challenges current theories of planet formation.

courtesy JPL-Caltech, NASA

This amazingly precise technology (despite an unfortunate technical hitch on board Kepler, which NASA is still scratching its head over) has enabled us to bring the tally of known extrasolar planets to around 3000, as of mid-2014, with many more unconfirmed and the number increasing by the week as more data are processed. There are thousands more candidates awaiting confirmation. This despite the fact that Kepler can only find planets whose orbits happen to be exactly edge on to us, a tiny fraction of the total.

The findings so far have enabled scientists to estimate that there could be as many as 40 billion planets of approximately the same size as Earth orbiting within the habitable zones of their parent stars within our own galaxy. The observable universe contains at least 100 billion galaxies, which gives us a total figure (if the Milky Way is at all typical) in the region of 4000 quintillion planets (4000 million million million).

THE LIMITS OF SPACE TRAVEL

If only we could hop on board a spaceship and go and take a look at some of the nearer ones. Unfortunately, real life is not like Star Trek. The prospects for travelling across interstellar space to visit other solar systems are not looking good.

A conventional spacecraft running on chemical fuel like the current generation of space probes would take around 70,000 years to reach the nearest star and over a hundred million years to cross the galaxy. Even with a tenfold or a hundredfold improvement in performance, this is so

Zark's Factoid...
At a maximum speed of about 17,600 mph, it would have taken a Space Shuttle about 165,000 years to reach Alpha Centauri.

hopelessly slow that it isn't even worth thinking about for interstellar missions. There are massive issues involved in sending people into space for longer than a few months, and long-term suspended animation on board a 'sleeper ship' is another invention of science fiction which does not look feasible in reality.

Perhaps we could send mini-colonies of people away in huge ships, to live, breed and die on board, so that centuries hence, after many generations, their descendants would eventually arrive at a distant world. Trouble is, it would take millennia rather than centuries, and the chances of the ship and its occupants arriving safely and actually carrying out the original plan are so small that the idea is barely worth considering.

But perhaps the paltry human lifespan of 80 years or so is not a drawback shared by aliens? Perhaps other advanced species live for centuries, even thousands of years? (After all, human lifetimes in developed countries have been increasing before our eyes, with the number of centenarians currently doubling every 13 years). If you were going to live for a thousand years, spending a few decades on board a spaceship might not seem such a daunting prospect.

No doubt this would help, but we have to remember the way

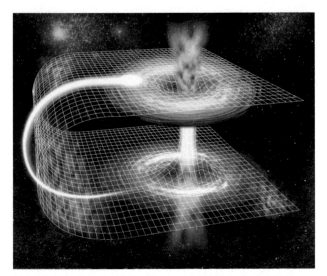

A feature of spacetime that can be viewed as a 2D surface and when 'folded' over a wormhole bridge would formed with at least two mouths which are connected to a single throat or tube.

to be a race against time. The generation period needs to be as short as possible – as indeed it is; everywhere we look we see animals developing, growing and breeding as quickly as their complexity allows.

Once any animal has bred and passed on its genes, nature has effectively finished with it, and it drifts into old age. Most animals die as soon as they are no longer fast and strong enough to compete for food. Human society enables us to live on to enjoy our declining years, and presumably this would happen with other intelligent species, perhaps more so, but nature still catches up soon enough. So although other advanced races are likely to have long lifespans, perhaps longer than ours, the chances are that they do not live for centuries or millennia.

WILL THE FUTURE PROVIDE THE ANSWER?

Whether extraterrestrial species live longer than us or not, surely they will have developed technologies which are beyond 21st century human comprehension, technologies which may well enable them to hop across galaxies in less time than it takes to say 'beam me up, Scotty'. Who's to say what an alien race a million years more advanced than us might have discovered?

evolution works. Each 'improvement' to an organism is built by selection pressure working with tiny, generation-by-generation changes, which means that for life to get all the way from an amoeba to an atomic physicist, many millions of generations are needed. For this to happen during the few billion years (at best) when conditions on a planet are suitable for life, there has

Many science fiction writers and alien enthusiasts espouse this view, yet the truth is that most of their ideas for space travel simply contravene the basic laws of physics, and we understand those laws very well. Gravity shields (wonderfully adopted by H G Wells in *The First Men In The Moon*) could never work, because gravity isn't some form of stuff that can be screened off, it's a fundamental property of spacetime and nothing is exempt from it. Drawing energy from the quantum vacuum would be no good either, because it represents the fall-back low energy state of the universe, and you need a difference in potential energy before you can draw some off. Wormholes – tiny, short-lived ones - exist deep within the equations of general relativity, but are almost certainly impossible in the sense used by sci-fi writers.

RELATIVITY TO THE RESCUE

One cunning, if challenging, possibility is that we could use one of the consequences of Einstein's other famous work, his Theory of Special Relativity. Suppose we found a power source which was so potent that we could accelerate a spacecraft as hard as we wanted for as long as we wanted, without running out of fuel. Current technology requires obscene quantities of

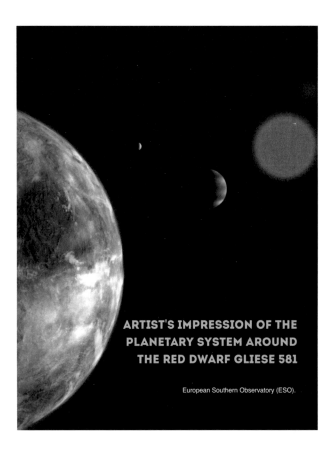

ARTIST'S IMPRESSION OF THE PLANETARY SYSTEM AROUND THE RED DWARF GLIESE 581

European Southern Observatory (ESO).

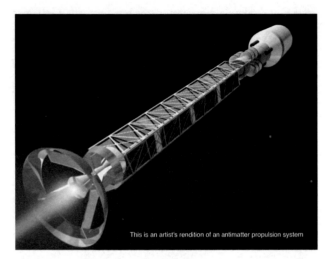

This is an artist's rendition of an antimatter propulsion system

Imagine the ship was headed for the star Gliese 581, 20 light years away in the constellation Libra (Gliese 581 has attracted a great deal of attention because it is relatively close to the Earth and has been found to have several planets orbiting it, a couple of which appear to be small terrestrial-type planets). The ship sets off, accelerating at a constant 1g (about 10 metres per second per second), which is ideal for the astronauts because once it has left the bonds of Earth the effect of that acceleration would mimic and replace Earth gravity.

At this rate our ship would take almost a year to reach the speed of light. Of course no massive object can exceed or even quite reach light's speed of 186,300 miles per second, but once the ship was travelling close enough to light speed, time on board would all but stop. The astronauts would be around half a light year from Earth (their average speed so far having been about half light speed), and they would agree with ground control that the first year or so of the journey had indeed taken 12 months. After that, however, their perception of events would be very different. The controllers would watch (if they could) for the next 19 or so years as the ship covered the

chemical energy and the production of vast amounts of waste heat just to heave a spaceship off the Earth's surface and get it into orbit. Theoretical solutions such as nuclear pulse propulsion and nuclear fusion, even an antimatter drive, would be much faster, but it would still take centuries to travel between stars. However, if we could somehow find a way of accelerating a spacecraft close to the speed of light, something very interesting would happen - time itself would alter.

Zark's Factoid...

After a six-month stint on the ISS, returning astronauts are just a tiny bit younger than the rest of us. Giving them 0.007 seconds of extra life.

bulk of the journey (the next 19 light years) at just under light speed. But on board the ship, those years would seem to fly by in days, hours, even minutes, depending on just how close to the speed of light the ship was travelling.

The last leg of the journey is a mirror image of the first, as the ship turns round through 180 degrees and spends the final year decelerating at 1g to landing speed. Upon touchdown, to the controllers, a little more than 21 years has passed; to the astronauts, it was barely two.

By the time the travellers have spent a few months surveying the planets of Gliese 581 and saying hello to the natives, and returned to Earth with their pictures, samples and souvenirs (assuming they do come back, of course), they will be around five years older than when they set off. But back at base, they will find that the mission control team who waved them off have long since retired, to be replaced by people who were not even born when they took off. They will be greeted by white-haired wives and husbands and children who are now older than they are.

There will be no reunion at all, of course, if the astronauts' ship happened to encounter even a tiny piece of cosmic debris on the way; when you hit something hard, however small, at near light speed, nothing is going to be left of you and your ship but a blinding flash and a cloud of gas.

John von Neumann

ROBOT SPACE EXPLORERS

If we are ever to colonise the galaxy, therefore, perhaps it will have to be done by robots. A self-replicating machine along the lines of the much-discussed von Neumann machine (proposed by mathematician John von Neumann in the 1940s) could take as long as it wanted over the journey from star to star. Upon arrival on a planet each machine could use the local mineral resources and energy from the parent star to build two copies of itself and despatch them to other solar systems. In this way, the whole galaxy could be colonised in a few tens of millions of years, depending on the speed of the probes. As far as we can see this hasn't happened, so if von Neumann machines work, it would appear that they have not been tried yet by anyone else in the galaxy. One more piece of evidence that intelligent life is rare – perhaps very rare indeed.

6

THE NEAR-MIRACLE OF LIFE ON EARTH

"FAR OUT IN THE UNCHARTED BACKWATERS OF THE UNFASHIONABLE END OF THE WESTERN SPIRAL ARM OF THE GALAXY LIES A SMALL, UNREGARDED YELLOW SUN. ORBITING THIS AT A DISTANCE OF ROUGHLY NINETY-TWO MILLION MILES IS AN UTTERLY INSIGNIFICANT LITTLE BLUE-GREEN PLANET WHOSE APE-DESCENDED LIFE FORMS ARE SO AMAZINGLY PRIMITIVE THAT THEY STILL THINK DIGITAL WATCHES ARE A PRETTY NEAT IDEA"

DOUGLAS ADAMS,
THE HITCHHIKER'S GUIDE TO THE GALAXY

Now to the big question – how far would we have to travel to find a planet with intelligent inhabitants? In recent years there has been much excitement about the number of 'terrestrial planets' or 'earths' which have turned up. These are convenient labels for the scientists, who simply mean that these planets are small enough to be rocky bodies which are likely to be broadly similar to Earth in size and composition. Many popular news media have been enthusiastically misled by this terminology, and have written about the latest new planets as if they were clones of the Earth in every respect, and almost bound to support intelligent life.

In fact, to support advanced life, such a planet would have to be much more than a rough copy of our own planet. It would have to share with it a number of subtle qualities, many of which are probably very unusual.

WHY LIFE IS A RACE AGAINST TIME

We've already seen how long it has taken Earth to produce advanced life forms. It's just as well it didn't take any longer, as our planet is running out of time.

The Sun and planets were born together 4.6 billion years ago, and the Sun's lifetime has been estimated at about nine billion years, so it is now halfway through. As its supply of nuclear fuel runs out, it is gradually getting hotter. Within about two billion years at most, it will have become so hot that the Earth's orbit will no longer be within the habitable zone of our solar system. Our beloved planet will dry out and eventually, as the Sun expands to reach its orbit or even further, it will be swallowed up in its dying fires.

Of course, whether there will be any trace of humankind left to suffer all this even a million years from now, let alone a billion, is entirely another matter. One thing's for sure - unless we have managed to make a new home further out in the solar system by then, or in another star system, all life on this planet will thereafter be a distant memory; not even that, as there will be probably be no one and nothing left to remember.

NO ORDINARY STAR

For many years the conventional wisdom about the Sun has been that by galactic standards it is just an ordinary boring old star. In fact there are several things about the Sun that are not at all ordinary.

SOME INTERESTING **SUN** FACTOIDS....

One million Earths could fit inside the Sun:
If a hollow Sun was filled up with spherical Earths then around 960,000 would fit inside.

Eventually, the Sun will consume the Earth:
When all the hydrogen has been burned, the Sun will continue for about 130 million more years, burning helium, during which time it will expand to the point that it will engulf Mercury and Venus and the Earth. At this stage it will have become a red giant

The Sun will one day be about the size of Earth:
After its red giant phase, the Sun will collapse, retaining its enormous mass, but occupying the approximate volume of our planet. When this happens, it will be called a white dwarf.

The Sun contains 99.86% of the mass in the Solar System:
The mass of the Sun is approximately 330,000 times greater than that of Earth. It is almost three quarters hydrogen, whilst most of the remaining mass is helium.

The Sun is an almost perfect sphere:
There is only a 10 kilometre difference in its polar diameter compared to its equatorial diameter. Considering the vast expanse of the Sun, this means it is the closest thing to a perfect sphere that has been observed in nature.

Light from the Sun takes eight minutes to reach Earth:
With a mean average distance of 150 million kilometres from Earth and with light travelling at 300,000 kilometres per second, dividing one by the other gives us an approximate time of 500 seconds, or eight minutes and 20 seconds. Although this energy reaches Earth in a few minutes, it will already have taken millions of years to travel from the Sun's core to its surface.

Bigger and brighter than you think:
It is actually bigger and brighter than the vast majority of stars. Around 95 per cent of the stars in the galaxy (and the universe) are smaller than the Sun

First, it is actually bigger and brighter than the vast majority of stars. Around 95 per cent of the stars in the galaxy (and the universe) are smaller than the Sun; only four of the 50 stars nearest to us are more massive. Most of these small stars are red dwarfs, which are inherently too variable to support life.

There's another problem with small stars, which is that their habitable zone will be too narrow for comfort. (The habitable zone of a planet is of course the area where the temperature remains compatible with life, which means where liquid water can persist.) Think of trying to keep warm by a camp fire on a desert night – you'd crowd as close as you could to get enough warmth, but your back would still be freezing.

Another difficulty with small stars is that their habitable zones may be so close in that a planet orbiting there would become tidally locked, with one face permanently towards the star, as has happened with the Moon in respect to the Earth.

This problem doesn't arise with stars that are bigger than the Sun, but instead we have another problem - bigger stars burn their fuel more quickly, which means there simply won't be time for advanced life to evolve on their planets before they fizzle out. As we'll see later, the Earth has needed all the time it could get to develop as far as it has.

COMFORTABLE ACCOMMODATION, WOULD SUIT SINGLE PLANET

The Sun is often said to have a habitable zone of a few tens of millions of miles, from somewhere outside the orbit of Venus to inside the orbit of Mars – plenty of room for two or even three life-bearing planets, you might think. But this hides a subtle point. Because the Sun, like most stars, is getting hotter as it gets older, its habitable zone is moving outward. For a planet to stay life-friendly for all the billions of years it seems to

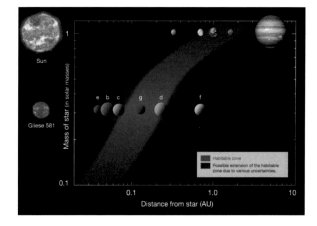

require to develop into intelligent beings, it has to remain, like Earth, in the 'continuously habitable zone' or CHZ – the area within which it *stays* habitable - for several billion years at a stretch. The CHZ for our solar system is thought to extend from just one million miles outside the Earth's orbit to about 5 million miles inside it. No wonder there isn't much sign of life on Mars or Venus.

An added complication is that a planet's temperature is affected by its atmosphere; the greenhouse gas effect keeps Earth several degrees warmer than it would otherwise be. Fortunately this extends the CHZ for our solar system out a little, but not by much.

So the Sun is just big enough to maintain a wide enough CHZ without burning its fuel too quickly and frying any life-bearing planets before they have time to develop their full potential.

AN EXCEPTIONALLY CONSTANT STAR

The sun's next key property as far as life are concerned is that its output remains almost exactly constant. Most stars are variable to some degree, certainly over millions of years; the Sun's output varies only by about 0.1 per cent in the short term (in time with the sunspot cycle), with slightly greater variation over centuries and millennia. Not only is its output steady, but the Earth's orbit around it is almost circular, so there is no significant warming or cooling effect from one part of the year to another (the seasons, of course, are caused by the tilt of the Earth's axis).

Finally, the Sun is of course on its own. Most stars form part of a binary or multiple system. Although it is not impossible for a planet to have a stable orbit in a continuously habitable zone around two suns, the chances of the whole shooting match remaining stable long enough for life to develop, even if a retinue of planets has formed, are slight.

A DESIRABLE NEIGHBOURHOOD

What about the Sun's position in the Milky Way? It turns out that this too is critical to the chances of life developing, for several reasons.

The Sun sits in a quiet backwater of our galaxy, well away from the turmoil of the galactic centre and between two of the spiral arms, so our neighbouring stars are far off and thinly scattered. This allows the solar system to lead a peaceful life, with very little trouble from the neighbours.

What sort of trouble are we talking about?

First, in crowded regions of a galaxy, close approaches between stars are much more likely. Such encounters will have disastrous consequences for their planets. Everything is ticking along very nicely in our solar system, with the planets trundling around in the same neat, near-circular orbits they have been following for billions of years. The arrival of another star within a trillion miles or so would well and truly put the cat among the pigeons. Its gravitation would have the same sort of effect on our planets as a tsunami on a fleet of fishing boats. Depending on the size of the star and the closeness of the approach, orbits would be severely disrupted, moons and planets would go careering past each other and in some cases, probably be flung out into interstellar space.

Such an event will be a regular occurrence, at least on cosmic time scales, in the more crowded regions of the galaxy. Out here in the sticks, we are pretty safe. We'll have to wait

Ahh... Peace & Quiet

well over a million years before another star (another from the Gliese catalogue, Gliese 710) will come a little too close for comfort. Although it will approach no closer than about a light year, even at this range its gravitational perturbation is likely to disturb the comets which orbit the Sun far out in the Oort Cloud*, and may send some of them plunging into the inner solar system, which could be interesting.

Secondly, the cosmic radiation which is so deadly to life is far more intense in the inner regions of the galaxy. Even our atmosphere might not save us if we were in the crowded inner regions of the Milky Way, within a few hundred light years of the deadly black hole that lies at its heart. Black holes themselves emit deadly bursts of radiation when they swallow gulps of captured matter. To be on a life-supporting planet, you don't want to be anywhere near a black hole.

Thirdly, every so often, our galaxy (like all galaxies) is lit up by a supernova; in fact one has just made headlines as I write this paragraph, in the nearby galaxy M82, which at about 12

The Oort Cloud is a region far outside the planetary zone of the solar system, extending as far as a light year from the Sun, where most of the comets live – probably billions of them. We only know the cloud is there because once in a while a comet from it, disturbed from its orbit by some cosmic interaction, comes whizzing in towards the Sun.

million light years away is one of our closest galactic neighbours. Even at that distance, the supernova in M82 could be seen, at its brightest in early February 2014, with binoculars. If you were unlucky enough to live on a planet orbiting a star within a few tens of light years of it, it would be time to say goodbye to all you hold dear; at that distance a supernova has enough energy to destroy most life on the surface of the Earth.

SUPERNOVAE – DESTROYERS AND CREATORS OF LIFE

So if our Sun had been born much closer to the centre of the galaxy, catastrophes of one kind or another would have come along too frequently for life to survive as it has for billions of years. If on the other hand it had been much further out, it would never have got started in the first place, because life needs heavy elements, and the old stars of the outer regions of the galaxy simply don't contain worthwhile amounts of any elements heavier than iron. Why do we have enough heavy elements for life, and they don't? Ironically (forgive the pun) it's because of the supernovae themselves.

That's because most of the heavier elements upon which life depends are actually created inside supernovae. We heard

SN 1994D (bright spot on the lower left), a type Ia supernova in the NGC 4526 galaxy

earlier that almost all of the universe is made up of a few simple elements, the most abundant (in order) being hydrogen, helium, oxygen, neon, nitrogen and carbon. Only the first two of these existed immediately after the Big Bang. The elements in the periodic table which follow, from oxygen up to iron, with its 26 protons, were all formed inside stars, by a process called stellar nucleosynthesis. All the elements beyond iron, from cobalt to uranium, have been created primarily inside supernovae. Without supernovae, we would not exist.

Specifically, the key to life is a Type 2 supernova, the kind you get when a star which is bigger than about twelve times the mass of the Sun explodes. This is a rare event on a human scale, but common enough by cosmic standards (there is very roughly about one a century in the Milky Way). The explosion is so violent that for a few weeks the star shines as brightly as a billion Suns, eventually collapsing into a tiny neutron star with all the space between the subatomic particles squeezed out, producing a density trillions of times that of normal matter. Unbelievably, a speck of the star's material the size of a grain of sand would weigh as much as a jet aircraft.

So great are the forces created by a Type 2 supernova that during the blast the combinations of protons and neutrons which form the elements up to iron are forced into contact, 'cooking' all the heavier elements in one unimaginably

The Crab Nebula is the remnant of SN 1054, a supernova (Type II) that was first observed on 4 July 1054 (hence its name), and that lasted for a period of around two years. In 1928, Edwin Hubble was the first to note that the changing aspect of the Crab nebula, which was growing bigger in size, suggests that it is the remains of a stellar explosion. He realised that the apparent speed of change in its size signifies that the explosion which it comes from occurred only nine centuries ago.

Crab Nebula by Hubble Space Telescope · Credit: NASA/ESA.

fierce melting pot. By the time the dust has settled, the supernova has created all the other 66 naturally-occurring elements. They are blasted out into space and spread around, eventually getting mixed up with the protostellar discs we heard about earlier.

Because these heavy elements are strewn around more and more widely as the aeons pass, new stars are born richer and richer in heavy metals as the universe ages. The outlying reaches of our galaxy, and the spectacular globular clusters which decorate its outskirts, are probably barren of life, because none of the stars out there have enough of the basic building blocks – the heavy elements. The Sun, in fact, is an exceptionally metal-rich star by comparison with most others we have examined. Some galaxies are thought to have no metal-rich stars at all and hence, if our theories are correct, are probably lifeless.

So if our Sun had started life when the universe was much younger, the solar system would not have had the elements necessary for life. And just as it has taken several billion years for animal life to arise in the solar system, it took several billion years before that for a star with the potential for life-bearing planets to be created in the first place. Life really does seem to need an awful lot of time to reach its full potential.

EARTH – A PLANET IN A BILLION

So much for the Sun and the special place it has in the galaxy, without which life could not have arisen. What about the solar system, and the Earth itself?

Although we now believe that most stars have planets, the presence of rocky ones like the Earth, in roughly the right orbit, depends on a few things going right. First of all, stars don't form in the middle of nowhere – they are born in crowded star nurseries where a great deal of gas and dust is concentrated together. This means that in the early millennia of a star's life it is likely to come into close contact with some of its broodmates before they all disperse, getting jogged, jostled and swung around. A close encounter with a bigger star in its early years could rob a star like the young Sun of the disc of dust and rock which it will need to make planets.

If that doesn't happen, the star and its disc of material drifts out into quieter regions. Assuming a companion star is not tagging along with it to queer the pitch, the scene is set for everything to settle down and for planets to form.

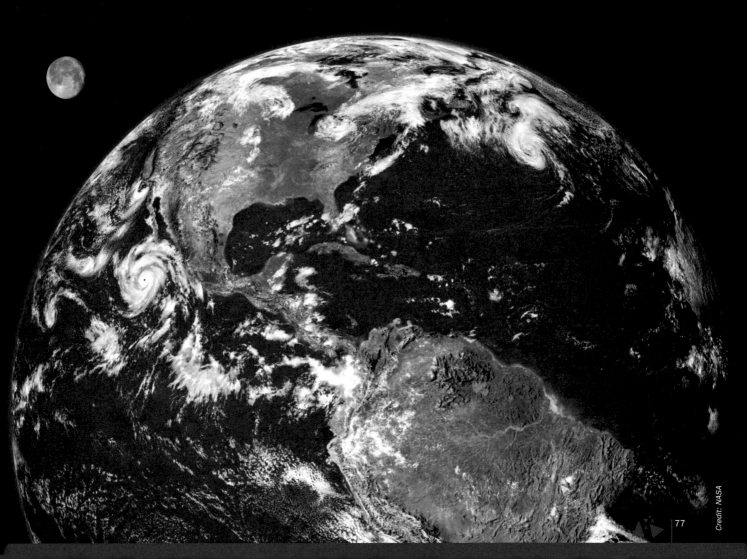

Credit: NASA

SOLAR SYSTEM SNOOKER

Computer simulations show that ordered solar systems like ours are a rarity. When scientists at Northwestern University in the USA repeatedly ran simulations featuring a newborn star like the Sun surrounded by a disc of gas and dust, they found that almost everything emerged except what we actually have. They concluded that conditions had to be just right for a solar system like ours to emerge.

While many aspects of our theories of planetary formation are still sketchy, the scientists have concluded that there are quite a few unusual features about ours.

For one thing, the position of Jupiter is a puzzle. Why is it way out in the sticks, 500 million miles from the Sun, when most of the other large planets we have found are much closer in? Theories of planetary formation have planets spiralling their way in through the gas and dust to wind up very close to the parent star, but this hasn't happened to Jupiter.

You might imagine that Jupiter is of no great importance to Earth, sitting as it does more than 400 million miles away from us at its closest, but in fact its presence is another factor without which life here would probably have had a rough ride. This is because it acts as a sort of giant goalkeeper for all the penalty shots the rest of the solar system throws at us.

Image of Comet Shoemaker–Levy 9 fragments (total: 21), taken on May 17, 1994

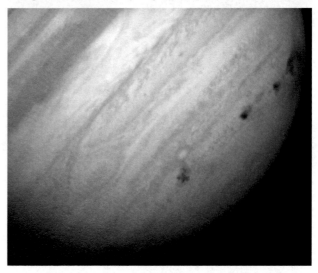

Brown spots mark impact sites on Jupiter's southern hemisphere.

Its enormous size and gravitational power compared to the other planets enables it to sit effortlessly fielding missiles which would otherwise plunge towards the Sun, subjecting us to far more cosmic impacts and far more extinction events than we actually experience. In 1994 we were able to see this process in action when the comet Shoemaker-Levy 9 plummeted into Jupiter before our eyes; a rare event on human timescales, but over the billions of years of Earth's history this must have happened countless times.

Major extinctions on Earth, some of them undoubtedly caused by impacts from large meteorites (asteroids), would have been far more numerous throughout Earth's history without Jupiter at the gate. As it is, global disaster seems to have struck about once every hundred million years or so since animal life appeared on Earth, and presumably before that, though the evidence of earlier impacts has long since disappeared. Life has been able to pick itself up, dust itself down and carry on after each of these, but if the bombardment had been much worse it's quite possible that on at least one occasion, disaster would have been total. A really severe impact from a big asteroid would wipe out everything living, forcing life on our planet to start all over again.

Yet Jupiter could just as easily – perhaps more easily – have been our nemesis instead of our saviour. From our observations of extrasolar planets so far, most Jovian (Jupiter-like) planets move much closer into their stars than ours has, gravitationally pushing the inner planets before them. If this had happened to us, Earth would have wound up much too close to the Sun for life to ever get started.

A MOON IN A MILLION

Our Moon is an enigma. Why is it so big in relation to its planet – around a quarter the diameter of the Earth? What is such a large moon doing in the inner solar system in the first place? Venus and Mercury don't have a moon between them, and Mars has just a pair of small, irregularly-shaped chunks of rock (Phobos and Deimos) which have clearly been captured at random. How did our Moon ever form?

Just as well it did, because without the benign presence of the Moon it seems advanced life on Earth would never have become established – that's how critical it is. This suggests that Earth-like planets elsewhere in the universe are going to have the same problem. Let's see why.

THE ACCIDENT THAT MADE THE MOON

Astronomers believe the Moon was created 4.4 billion years ago, in the very early days of the solar system, by a collision between Earth and a hypothetical nearby planet dubbed Theia, around the size of Mars, which had presumably formed in the same orbit. When the two collided, both were reduced to molten rock and metal. Their metallic cores combined and their rocky mantles merged on top to form a new and bigger planet – Earth. However some of the splashed-out surface material got left over and began to orbit the new combined planet in fragments, gradually coalescing to form the Moon. The fact that the Moon lacks an iron core (the Earth has a large one), but is otherwise made of exactly the same stuff as Earth, is strong evidence that it was made from part of the Earth's mantle.

So how did the Moon help the Earth to develop advanced life?

First of all, the impact with Theia is thought to be responsible for the Earth's rapid rotation – around five hours at first, slowing over the ages to the 24 hours we are familiar with today. Combined with that iron core, part of which is also down to the collision with Theia, this has given the Earth an unusually strong magnetic field. The field creates the magnetosphere, a magnetised zone which extends many thousands of miles from the planet's surface and deflects harmful particles from the Sun and elsewhere in space, such as electrically-charged protons and high-energy cosmic rays.

Periodically, at random intervals (every half a million years or so, on average) the Earth's magnetic field weakens, disappears, and then starts up again polarised in the opposite direction. During these periods the magnetosphere fades away, and the fossil record shows us that each time it happens, an unusual number of creatures become extinct. This is evidence that without the magnetosphere, advanced life would probably never have got going.

Second, the Moon keeps the rotation of the Earth stable. The fact that our planet's axis of rotation is tilted at 23 degrees to the plane of its orbit (another result of the impact with Theia) is responsible for the seasons. We know from our observations of other planets, notably Mars, that their tilts are unstable and can suddenly (on cosmic timescales) change dramatically. If this happened to Earth, its delicately-balanced climates would be plunged into chaos. During periods when it was lying on its side, the poles would alternately be fried and frozen, creating huge extremes of climate and making life very difficult. Only the constant gravitational tug of the Moon stops this happening.

The one lunar effect we all know about of course is the twice-daily tides the Moon causes (with a little help from the Sun). It is likely that at the time when life was getting established on land, these tides came in very handy. By creating a transitional inter-tidal zone as they still do today, they will have provided the ideal environment for aquatic creatures to spend part of their time out of water, en route to evolving into terrestrial animals as we know they did.

THE KEY ROLE OF CONTINENTAL DRIFT

Alfred Wegener

It's only a few decades since scientists finally accepted that the ideas of a maverick early twentieth-century scientist called Alfred Wegener were right; the surface of the Earth is not as fixed and rigid as it appears. It is built up of a series of thin rocky plates floating on the denser liquid mantle and constantly moving in relation to one another. In some places two plates are grinding along edge to edge, while in others one edge is pushing below another. It is at these 'subduction zones' that volcanoes emerge, while the grinding edges are responsible for the most destructive earthquakes, when the two edges

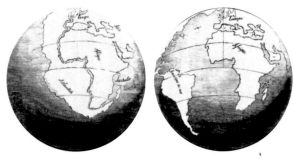

First known illustration of the opening of the Atlantic Ocean, by Antonio Snider-Pellegrini, 1858.

suddenly slip past one another by a few metres. Thanks to plate tectonics, as it's known, the continents are all slowly wandering about, on a timescale of many millions of years; 130 million years ago, Europe was joined to what is now North and South America.

Plate tectonics and continental drift only happen when you have just the right ingredients. That means a thin rocky crust floating on a liquid mantle in which material is circulating by convection, plus an ocean to lubricate the process and soften the rock. There is no plate tectonics on Venus or Mars, or indeed anywhere else in the solar system.

So why is plate tectonics important to life? For one thing, we now believe that the process acts as a global thermostat, a way of keeping a planet's temperature constant. This is because, through what is known as the CO_2-silicate cycle, carbon dioxide is constantly being absorbed into the oceans and then locked up in sedimentary rocks. Eventually the rocks release it again through weathering and volcanic activity. The process works faster when a planet warms up and slows down when it gets cold, so it acts as a buffer against extremes of temperature.

None of this would be possible if the ocean was too deep, or there was too little of it. Life would not get very far in any case on a planet with very little water (water being the nursery and cradle of all life, as far as we have learned), or with too much water. On a planet which is all ocean, life might get as far as it did on Earth, perhaps to creatures like fish and plesiosaurs. But we are not likely to hear from such a planet; it's hard to imagine a plesiosaur building a radio telescope.

It's also worth remembering that life here acquired much of its extraordinary variety through geographical separation. Charles Darwin's great moment of enlightenment about the process of evolution followed his visit to the Galapagos islands, where he saw how the finches of different islands had formed separate populations which had become differentiated from one another. This process would happen more slowly on a planet where the land was all linked together, and as we have learned, the evolution of advanced animals is a race against cosmic time.

So how come we have just the right amount of water?

Here's another piece of luck for the Earth. It's thought that our water came mainly from comets, 'dirty snowballs', which were much commoner in the solar system in its early days than they are now. In the millennia after its formation, Earth was bombarded with them – just enough of them to give it the ocean it needed, but not enough to drown the chances of life getting to the Times Crossword stage of evolution.

Nucleus of Comet 103P/Hartley as imaged during a spacecraft flyby. The nucleus is about 2 km in length.

The idea that Earth is a far more unusual planet than we have previously given it credit for, and that planets like it are going to be hard to come by in the universe, is known as the Rare Earth Hypothesis (for a detailed and fascinating account, see *Rare Earth* by Peter D Ward and Donald Brownlee). They suggest a new version of the Drake Equation we read about in chapter 2:

$$N = N^* \times fp \times fpm \times ne \times ng \times fi \times fc \times fl \times fm \times fj \times fme$$

In this version the symbols denote the following:

N =   the number of civilisations now active in the Milky Way

N^* =   the number of stars in our galaxy

fp =   the fraction with planets

fpm =   the fraction of planets which are metal-rich

ne =   number of planets in the average star's habitable zone

ng =   proportion of stars which are in a galaxy's habitable zone

fi =   fraction of habitable planets which have produced life

fc =   fraction of the above where complex animals arise

fl =   proportion of a planet's life when it is occupied by complex animals

fm =   the fraction of planets with a large moon

fj =   the fraction of solar systems with Jupiter-sized planets

fme=   the fraction of planets with a critically low number (safe frequency) of extinction events

While some of these numbers can be entered with reasonable confidence, others, notably fc and fm, appear unknowable. We can only make wild guesses.

Ward and Brownlee have not attempted to put values on any of these figures, but you can have fun doing it yourself. Chances are you will wind up with a very small number indeed. The astrophysicist and science writer John Gribbin, in *Alone in the Universe* (2011), makes a bolder claim: "The Milky Way contains a few hundred million stars, but almost certainly only one intelligent civilisation… we are alone, and we had better get used to the idea".

7 EXTENDING THE HUNT FOR ALIEN LIFE

"WHEN WE THINK ABOUT ADVANCED ALIEN CIVILISATIONS, WE ARE ALSO GLIMPSING THE FUTURE OF MANKIND. THE EERIE SILENCE GIVES US PAUSE THAT SUCH A FUTURE IS BY NO MEANS ASSURED"

PAUL DAVIES, THE EERIE SILENCE

Put this book down and take a deep breath. If it is dark outside and the night is clear, go out into the garden, or to the nearest place where you can get away from the lights of civilisation, and look up. If you are lucky enough to be in an area where the air is not too polluted and it really is a clear night, you will see millions of stars. Actually it only seems like millions – from any spot you can only see about 4000 individual stars with the naked eye, though you should be able to see the silvery band of the Milky Way, which is of course composed of the light of billions more.

Surely, on a planet orbiting just one of those stars, there must be someone we could talk to?

Despite the considerable evidence for the Rare Earth Hypothesis and the realisation that only the minutest fraction of stars are likely to be orbited by planets bearing intelligent life, we also know that the universe is spectacularly big, possibly infinite. If it is infinite, it follows inescapably that not only is there an infinite number of alien intelligences out there, there is an infinite number of planets almost exactly like Earth; somewhere there must be an Earth clone on which everything is identical except for one word in this book, and another on which it's a different word. This is a seriously brain-hurting concept, but a human inability to comprehend something does not of course mean it can't happen. But even if the universe is not infinite, it is probably very, very big. The curvature of space has been measured as flat to very fine tolerances, which suggests that at the very least it goes way, way beyond what we can see.

So all hope of finding someone to talk to out there is not lost. It's just that we may have to travel impossible distances to find them. We've heard that crossing galaxies simply isn't on, unless some quite extraordinary new science emerges which makes it possible, such as wormholes (a theoretical possibility, though not of the size and duration that could allow people to pass through them) or faster-than-light travel. Unfortunately the latter really does seem to be impossible, and probably always will be.

WIDENING THE SEARCH

So what are we looking for? There is no way, however big our telescopes get, of seeing direct evidence of life on a planet circulating another star, even one relatively nearby. But there are clues which would betray it. The first of these is the atmosphere; the mixture of nitrogen, oxygen and water vapour we have on Earth would never arise, let alone persist, on a dead planet. If our spectroscopes ever tell us that we have found an Earth-like atmosphere on a distant planet, we may regard that as pretty strong evidence for the existence of plants at least, as oxygen is produced and maintained only through photosynthesis.

Measuring telltale signals like this of life on Earth-like planets within the habitable zones of their stars is a formidable challenge technically – seen from a distance, the Sun is about a billion times brighter than the Earth - but it is not impossible, and it will get easier as our technology develops.

We may just have to fall back on looking for radio messages – which is where we came in.

A FOR ANDROMEDA

In 1961 the astronomer Sir Fred Hoyle, who became famous for several achievements, most notably his work on stellar nucleosynthesis, wrote a TV serial and a science fiction novel called *A For Andromeda*. The story, which was inspired by the inception of Project Ozma (see chapter 2), begins when a group of scientists working in a remote research station in the north of England receive a strange radio message from a star two hundred light years away in the Andromeda constellation. They decode the message and follow the instructions contained in it, which eventually enable them to 'grow' in the laboratory a beautiful young woman (she was played on television by Julie Christie in her debut screen role). The girl is apparently human, but of course, she is too good (and too beautiful) to be true – she is actually the agent of an alien race. Hoyle was an excellent storyteller as well as a renowned scientist, and it's a wonderful yarn, based (unlike most of the sci-fi of the period) on real science. It could happen.

A For Andromeda reminds us that aliens don't have to master space travel to colonise other worlds. They can simply broadcast instructions to build clones of themselves on far-off planets, enabling them to colonise the universe at the speed of light. Whether they would actually want to do this is impossible to know; all we do know is that life is built on the constant urge to self-replicate. It has to be, or it wouldn't exist.

Looking on the bright side, messages like that one, and the rather similar storyline in Carl Sagan's *Contact*, in which instructions are sent to build a machine for travelling through space, might actually turn up. No new physics is required. We are already listening; all we have to do is keep at it. We might have to wait a million years (or forever), or the longed-for signal might show up next week.

Radio signals from space may be the only way we are ever going to find out about other civilisations. And because life forms which have developed technology are probably very rare, it really does look, as Hoyle's character John Fleming said in *A For Andromeda*, as if those messages are going to come from 'a long way out'.

WHAT IF WE HEAR FROM ET?

Just suppose that one day, the dream of all ufologists and sci-fi lovers and many scientists comes true – we get a real live message from the stars. What would we do about it?

The message could simply be a greeting, or an invitation to join some kind of cosmic radio telescope owners' club. But as the senders will know that there is no hope of bouncing messages back and forth across the light years, it is going to have to be a one-off, one-way-only communication, so the chances are that it will be a great deal more substantial than a simple 'Hi there, just thought we'd get in touch'. It may be

packed with so much information that it will take us years to decode and translate.

Perhaps the message will be a warning: 'Stop trashing your planet and killing each other', or 'There's a comet heading your way, get out while you can'. But from hundreds of light years away, how they are going to know, until long after the event?

LESSONS FROM THE STARS

A more constructive idea is that we might get a message from a dying race that wish to pass on their technical and scientific knowledge to the rest of the cosmos before succumbing to the fires of a dying sun. That would be fascinating - perhaps terrifying. Could we cope with all that knowledge? Are we mature enough to learn more than we already know about how to mess with our environment? It would certainly create fierce competition between nations for all that new technology.

Perhaps it would be better if an advanced civilisation contacted us to tell us how they had overcome the challenges of war and conflict and learned how to live peacefully without damaging the world around them. That would be evidence that it can be done; it would be even more helpful if they sent some instructions for following their example. The hard part would be to spread the word and get the rest of humanity to listen, instead of dismissing it as just another pile of religious claptrap. Most humans are not, unfortunately, chiefly motivated by a desire for world peace.

On the evidence to date, this galaxy is not humming with intelligent life, to say the least. Alien beings with calculators and telescopes are probably fabulously rare. But the more we learn about the universe, the more confident we can be that they ought to be out there somewhere, and if they are, there is hope that one day, we will hear from them.

RECOMMENDED READING

Are We Being Watched?, Paul Murdin, Thames & Hudson 2013

Alien Universe, Don Lincoln, Johns Hopkins University Press 2013

The Eerie Silence, Paul Davies, Penguin 2011

Alone In The Universe, John Gribbin, John Wiley 2011

The Fallacy of Fine Tuning, Victor J Stenger, Prometheus 2011

We Are Not Alone, Dirk Schulze-Makuch and David Darling, Oneworld 2010

Rare Earth, Peter D Ward and Donald Brownlee, Copernicus 2004

Life's Solutions, Simon Conway Morris, Cambridge University Press 2003

The Universe Next Door, Marcus Chown, Headline 2002

ND - #0037 - 270225 - C96 - 148/210/5 - PB - 9781861511126 - Gloss Lamination